PARTIAL SHADE

John Birtwhistle was born in Scunthorpe in 1946. He received
an Eric Gregory Award in 1975 and ten years later his
third book was a Poetry Book Society Recommendation.
Nearly all his work has been supported by public money,
whether through education as a Lecturer in English at the
University of York, or through Arts Council funding of books,
fellowships and opera, or through the NHS income of his wife
Mireille. Since 1992, he has lived in Sheffield with his family.
He is working on a new collection of poems, and on a book
about poets confronting death.

Partial Shade

POEMS NEW AND SELECTED

John Birtwhistle

CARCANET POETRY

First published in Great Britain in 2023 by
Carcanet
Alliance House, 30 Cross Street
Manchester, M2 7AQ
www.carcanet.co.uk

A CIP catalogue record for this book is
available from the British Library.

ISBN 978 1 80017 323 1

Book design by Andrew Latimer, Carcanet
Typesetting by LiteBook Prepress Services
Printed in Great Britain by SRP Ltd, Exeter, Devon

The publisher acknowledges financial
assistance from Arts Council England.

With gratitude
to my editor-publishers
through many years

PETER JAY

MICHAEL SCHMIDT

CONTENTS

III

IV

VIII

FOREWORD

I see from the radiocarbon dating that my first collection of poems came out in 1972. There are many ways of selecting over such a period, none of them right or wrong, so I should explain that the book in your hands is not a chronological selection from previous books in order of publication. Nor does it tell a life story in order of composition. Rather, I have treated the body of work as though I had been asked by a stranger to look through a bag of loose anonymous undated papers in the hope of shaping some of them into a book.

I have found eight thematic groupings. This owes less to any Selected Poems formula than it does to the art of Anthology, which arranges materials from a variety of times and authors. I have listened for conversation across and against the years, moods and forms. The somewhat longer poems in sections IV and VI are interludes in this arrangement.

In a few cases, I have excerpted or revised for this book (even altering a few titles). The first publication of each poem is noted in the Acknowledgements. And in a Carcanet Blog I have gone into more detail about the reasons and motives (I can hardly say principles) by which these poems have been selected, edited and arranged.

I

THE FLOWERING CURRANT

As though from the Chinese

1
The linnet sings
The bullrush stands again
Grey water blues again at the brim

The storm flakes out
Only the watcher is troubled still

2
Today received several complaints
issued few instructions
forgot about verse

Dark finds me studying
another paper alone

3
My duties take care of themselves
Decisions are made elsewhere
Many would say I ought to be content

to breathe these orange-flowers
filled with memories

4
An inner courtyard
silently walls in
your absence with a disused well

I gaze from my desk
embezzling time

5
I joke somewhat stiffly
Colleagues wonder
Has he a heart in his ribs?

My heart may tremble
My back is a yardstick

6
Much of the afternoon
when I should be writing reports
I draft these lines on willow leaves

as they fall sharp
in patterns on the many paths

7
The first official
day of spring finds me
collecting fines

and the longstemmed
flowering currant in flower

8
I get noticed for the willow verse
Larger matters are not in my gift
The willow curves in its own script

Eye for detail has the say
in offices like mine

9
In this courtyard
a famous dialogue is set
and we discussed it here

Duty keeps calling me back
where I can look out for you

10
Silky sky
haze of pollen
are bringing back my thoughts

Once we were candid
and cast a single shade

11
As the peartree fails
and friends drop away
it is often the slightest things

Child's play with pebbles
The scent of rain long delayed

12
My young colleague passes
a newborn son
round the table like a cheese

wishing him nothing but brains
which have done so much for us

13
Having once passed exams
l can sit at this table
tracing name after name

and absently look up at the wall
and name what frightens me

14
Press gangs
go with my seal
along the springline villages

though l would rather protect
the poor of this world

15
l dreamed again
of the slight field
in the small of the hill

as though the edge could keep
when the knife is melted down

16
Horsemen muster on the plain
Stupid birds will soon be setting out
where I am forbidden to go

longing for here
where I used to hear you laugh

17
A brace of duck
beck and call
neither calling first

The sun a crimson seal
The lake a cleaned mirror

18
In another room
someone cuts fennel
an entrancing smell

Whole provinces pass
into other hands

19
Horsemen return
Several villages
a single plume of smoke

Even at my desk
winter sets in

20
Sick leave enables
me to linger for once
with the hundred poets

those of dispassion
those of inmost thought

21
Being reliable
I know what it means
to pass on orders

Being liable
I know what exile means

22
By a single taper
I write out an old verse
I would care to have written

dwelling on love
that bookish theme

23
Dusk
a frail bridge
I cannot put you out of mind

A skein of geese
Mist rising from the lake

24
Clear stars only recall
the alterable things
as I lie with my thoughts

Elsewhere in the house
a child cries with my voice

25
In the presence of others
you touched me on the wrist
Woken early by messages my dreams

go on and I wonder how you are
somewhere beyond in the morning

FOR ONE NIGHT ONLY

As I walked alone at night on Port Meadow
She revealed herself as a frail curtain,
The merest breeze gently wavering between
Greenish and pink, so I had to exclaim:
Though so far south, you are the famous Aurora!

I was magnetised by the fold and flow of fabric
As though clinging to the limbs of a goddess
Whose descendant the very next day I enticed
To walk with me at the same place and time
In impious promise of Her apparition again.

SOLE PROPRIETOR

The door of her darkened shop
where no one seems to buy
(perhaps it's time to give up)

is her viewing pavilion

a door to that afternoon when he
showing off to her
climbed a tree to unsnag a kite.

THE ENGLISH CEMETERY IN FLORENCE
After Franco Fortini

Evening, October
and even now
    through the avenues the mist
        lightly
    veils the plane trees
as in those times of ours
walled in ivy and cypress.

The keepers
are burning twigs and dry laurels.
                  Greenish the smoke
like that from charcoal burners
                      in the mountains.

They would die,
    those evenings, already chill
                and I would search
    for your wrist to stroke.
Then were the uncertain lights
the large shadows of gardens
and your firm step on the gravel

and the stone at the iron gates
       you used to say
had the smell of October in it
and the smoke had a breath of the vintage
and your mouth
       opened itself in the dark
             a slow yielding grape.

And now perhaps I would not recognise
                    your form.

I suppose you are alive
                    and think sometimes

of how much passed between us

and how much is passed

                    And from time to time
a longing such as may sigh in the dead

                    to go back
            to look again
        on the one you used to be

walking in those evenings of a time
which has no place

            even though
                even now
I am walking down these avenues of Florence
                where the mist
                lightly
                veils the plane trees

and in the gardens burn
the laurel fires.

A SWALLOW
For David Blake

Year after year a swallow tries to nest
on the self-same balcony.
Year after year the housewife clears it out
only to find that speck of lime.

How can the swallow remember a time
when it was not unwelcome
on that balcony facing south
where year after year it still tries to nest?

THE CORE

The wall I see from my desk where a core
thrown aside has become a blossoming tree
an apple core thrown by the wall
becoming as though to read my thoughts
a small bearing tree
noticed by passers-by who scrump
an apple or share to their friends
its blossom in Spring

shows me this morning a woman so
magnificently pregnant and also
defenceless with laughter
at some story her man insists on telling her
that she has to lean
quaking against the appletree wall. Here's!
to the accident that chucked that core.

WEDDING SONG
For Pam and Nick

True Birds of Paradise
Never alight or nest
But wing unflaggingly
Throughout the vacant skies
Touching no stone or tree.

If so, let us be false
And take our colours from
Flowers that make their show
In a bird's likeness but
Strike harder roots below.

Grounded, let us delight
In all that draws a stem
From soil of actual things.
Admire the petal's beak.
Observe the annual rings.

LINES PINNED TO A STUDY DOOR

Mireille

When first I read in cunning Chaucer's line
The lyf so short, the craft so long to lerne
I took the gist for poetry and mine,
The reader's smile so troublesome to earn.

The entrance to your hospital engraves
An ageless maxim of Hippocrates –
ARS LONGA VITA BREVIS – as it braves
The cure for this, our bodies' brief disease.

One phrase distills our art and oath,
A lifelong study for us both.

II

RIDDLE OF THE SKIN

As I print out your body lying under mine
You could read my lines who,
Being as deep as your beauty, twist
Into so many faces for your friends.
I feel for you in sleet and fire.
I handle your goods and chattels.
I am duly touched by your family.
You and I are all but inseparable
Although a hiding could scare me away.
Forfend that you that thinks I'm you
Should see yourself, raw as you are.
No thinking but I contain it.
No thinking when I turn to wax.
Without me, your body's bandage,
Mankind is but a walking wound.

AT SWINE STY

The valley turns, and in this hollow
the breeze has fallen. A lark descends.
The fragrant bracken is nearly still.
A solitary foxglove hardly sways.
Deertracks converge in shelter.
High and around are Bronze Age fields
abandoned to the sky.
All the senses will have been so then.
                              How voices carry!

AN ARCHAEOLOGIST EXPLAINS A SCAR

This shallow bowl's ineffaceable trace
was not just another charcoal-burner's pit:

mounded along this side, depleted over there
from soil being ripped up and transferred,

it is that a great tree once fell in these woods,
tearing to drag upright its webbed foot grasping

at stones, only to rot and release them over the years
to leave this crescent for us to interpret, exclaim

how mighty a column it was that long ago crashed
and how shallow it must always have been, in its roots.

JOHN BRADFORD, EXECUTED 1555

He that said   *There but for*
the Grace of God go I   went.

MINUTES OF THE LOOSE VILLAGE COTTAGE GARDENERS' SOCIETY: SELECTIONS FROM MANUSCRIPT IN MAIDSTONE MUSEUM

2nd November, 1910. The amount of fines,
usually distributed amongst Tenants whose
allotments have been best kept, is so small

as to be not worthy of division among
the faultless members. Your committee
are greatly disquieted by a rumour

of building Council Schools for the Parish
on a portion of the Allotments ground.
The first building erected on the grounds

will destroy security of tenure, inevitably
followed by a decline of interest and endeavour.
Obviously, the Allotments form the Society's

main bond of Union; and from other
points of view, the severance of this bond
would be a matter greatly to be deplored.

31st October, 1917. Twelve of our tenants
having joined H.M.'s Forces of War,
6 for home defence, 6 for Foreign Services,

your committee felt it their duty
to undertake on their behalf
the cultivation of the plots they held.

14th October, 1918. I have been for some time
anxiously considering the question
of a Memorial to our Loose heroes

who have fallen in the War. I have come
to the conclusion that a Memorial Hall
open to all classes and all denominations

would be the most suitable popular and useful
form of Memorial. A site would be required
and I think no better one could be had

than a small portion of the allotment ground.
31st October, 1918. This year is unquestionably
the most momentous of any in our lives.

The fierce and protracted struggle of Right against Wrong
has ended in Right emerging a crowned Victor.
With the Victory there dawns an advent of supreme justice;

and among the fruits of Victory will be
the provision of Allotments, for such as desire
and need them; with security of tenure.

FOR THE CHILD WHO GAVE MAYAKOVSKY
AN ORANGE, OCTOBER 1913

Lenses   gears   typographers' metal   sharp active
    particulars   Reflection is one with quickness
        Useful and insightful no longer a distinction

A man in a yellow coat adorning trains with slogans
    and the crowd on the canal-bridge whisper Look
        He's eating!   He's eating!   The reader is the word

A word is a bit of metal   Materials are ideas
    Dispersal of leaflets from train windows
        The lyricist a sloganeer   Revolution is a train

Hope unbuds its details packed to capacity
    Everyone the subject and object of experiment
the river low lying licking at rushes

brilliant as glass or metal   The audience is the play
    All buildings open to all   Cheap housing
        not cheap booze   The resurrection of the dead

Poetry is speech plus electricity   Tense up
    while reflected reeds are retracing our surface
        in a great co-motion of abstract and humane

Artistic standing with social   with the objective
    Intense intellectuality posted up in the streets
        Philosophies composed direct onto printing machines

or swans brinking abreast of the vapour
     and lectured in the Hall of the Society of Art Lovers
         on the drainpipe as a musical instrument

Individuality the flourishing of co-operation
     Every cog must grow ingenious   Dream is a textbook
        We are in the swim and brains are made of fish

a lock looking on in lack of a keeper
     'Are being shot'   Factories take over from icons
        Engineering is an art   Machines are natural

'The census is not to be published this year'
     The abstractions of art and science become
        the language of experience   *A tree appeals to reason*

ABOUT YEVTUSHENKO'S *BABI YAR*

Poetry, that could prevent
not a single happening
in the valley of shadows,
may sing against silence.

THE MARKET

It takes millions of years to petrify wood
by mineral infiltration of every cell.

       In a peasant market in Belgrade, I watched
a showman selling whetstones fashioned from
sharp silicate wood-like fibres, a spread of this
matter made up into short rods like so many
carrots. Onto each end, he had forced a length
of heat-softened hosepipe to grip the exact
surface of each piece of stone so as to make
a handle for each tool.

       On with the show.
First, he would noisily deaden the edge
of a pair of scissors with scrapes of the fossil
across each of its shears, then demonstrate
with coarse comedy the thing was now too dull
to cut even one of the squares of newspaper
of which he'd prepared a neat pile. The paper
just got trapped, hardly bruised, the scissors
flaccidly blunt.

       Next, with a flourish he seemed
to re-sharpen the scissors with a stick of his own
special wood and, picking up another square
of paper between thumb and forefinger, did not
even try to scissor it but sliced it through in
mid-air with one scissor blade, to show all was now
razor-sharp. Who would not buy such fossil wood?

I hung around for several performances
of his perfect pitch, admiring as one might
a conjurer but also thinking, had I to do this all day,
how might I set about it? Perhaps never blunt
the scissors – just appear to, with dramatic
swordplay (the pivotal rivet loosened
so edges could never engage). Then, for the
aerial display, have to my hand that blade,
ready-sharpened, as it might well have been,
by some private source of fossil wood.

                       So musing
sceptically, but also relishing his art, I was not
the only one to notice that, deliberately
or not, the very next square on the pile of news
happened to frame exactly a standard press
portrait of Tito.

           The watchers fell strangely
attentive, but the artist showed not the slightest
sign of clocking an icon. He followed routine
until that point where he would have slashed
the image on the next square of paper which,
however, without fuss, he carefully laid aside.

           Or so I remind in mineralising memory.

They are to be found in every known country.
The history of every hitherto   Damn that dog!
    for the duration of the emergency   Grief
How am I supposed to write with this?
    of the current threat   has gone and left
a young alsatian chained to a lintel
        and the shade has been moving round
        as the stress on 'torment' from noun to verb.
    for up to seven days without trial and with
Who will rid me of this turbulent beast?
throwing back his head and barking and barking
throughout the siesta   as their hopeless letters,
and for enquiring into each other's fate
    bounding against his chain.
                I could shoot
        Evidence that torturers are first tortured
        themselves   to make a brute of him, a guard
of a supple creature like that!   Without water
    sometimes leaving a scrap of paper, scratches
on the wall   It is insufferable, I just can't
of   anything but that infernal   on obscure charges
    of that shouting   a vicious education   in-turned
        And of how we laughed at him prancing
        about in the fans of the lawn-sprinkler
Who fell out of the window while in custody.
They've deserted you, get that into your head.
Lie down, sleep it out, you've enough chain.

A shutter goes up. Next all the balconies
are shouting at once and something will be,
maybe, done about him, being an animal
we can see and hear and which troubles our rest.

SIGINT

The silent aeroplane
a bulge on its forehead
the dolphin's melon

DESTINY

A heavy trailer parks up by the playground.
Boys, as they see their fathers and brothers do,
Kick at the tyres and twang the ropes on the load.

THE QUEEN'S SHILLING

Every year, when exam results are out
so are recruiting sergeants.
School-leavers hanging around
in the city centre, spending money
they don't have on girls they don't have,
are drawn to a camo Army tent
with a muted recruitment vid
like a game on pause to be played
as they're talked into safe-ish risks
by boy soldiers in combat gear.
This season, the camouflage style
is an effect of sunset on desert sand.

SEVENTH OF NOVEMBER, 1956
For Alan Brownjohn

        The sky was violent with shells
tracers and rockets, on Bonfire Night.
                Next evening, the boy
was indoors tweezing little rubber letters
into the slot of his John Bull Printing Outfit, snipping

rubber into moveable type and paper into strips,
getting confused between S and Z in mirror writing,
and stamping from his pad of violet ink.

              So in the morning
there he is at the school gate, standing like an orator
on a crate of third-pint milk bottles,
clenching his urgent sheaf and crying BUY
MY NEWSPAPER! ONLY A PENNY!

and, as street newsvendors do, bawling its headline
PORT SAID FALLS! PORT. SAID. FALLS!
Thus giving away, for free, the entire content
of his paper.

       I do not say that Richard Hughes
knew that he was in on the beginning of the end,
or what was then brewing with Russia
or on John Bull's Malayan rubber plantations

but I marvel yet that this fiery ten-year-old,
not content to impress his own name on his wrist
or make officious tickets for little performances

this red-headed boy whose message I did not buy

and whom even now I'm ashamed to have teased,
with his penny paper and his triumphant elegy
PORT   SAID   FALLS,   PORT   SAID   FALLS

was somehow aware that momentous matters
were on the move and the world of Green Lane
County Primary School had to be told that, in print.

EMBLEM
A memory of Sandy Cunningham

As I walked to work across the Common
a crow was pecking at a dead rabbit's eye

scared off by a dog who at once addressed
the same matter.

                    In the Common Room
I relate this 'medieval emblem
of bestiality'.

                You merely enquire,
'Why don't you say how human it all is?'

When us Pelagians ripped up cobblestones
in rue Gay-Lussac, that illustrious name
if noted at all was a schoolbench gripe
for all his indigo, balloon and methodical thought.

Did we not hear the beetle ticking in the beam?

Hence the button badge SCIENCE FOR THE PEOPLE
with red fist superimposed on white hand
holding a triangular flask, not more subtle
than the fist but recalling your inflected hand

the distillation of careful analysis
no less delicate than excellent scholars
inventing napalm to exact specification

But this was SCIENCE FOR THE PEOPLE

and I only ask whether that fist was aware
of that hand and why the design could not
marry them and how the tension went unnoticed

when in the standard shot from the door, down
the gunsights onto wooded hills, you spotted
the shot for a moment included the shadow
of the black dragonfly from which it was taken.

RINGS OF JADE
Versions from Ho Chi Minh

1

Borne by the stream
the boat glides on
my legs roped up
to a roofbeam gibbet

Along the banks
are thriving villages
as the fishing boat glides
midstream

2

Force-marched
thirty miles today
shirt soaking
shoes splitting

All night long
nowhere to lie
I wait for another day like this
hunched by a dungheap

3
Although my limbs
are tied well enough
I can hear the birds
and smell the woods in spring

Who can stop me
enjoying these
that take from a long trek some
of its loneliness?

4
Branches fretted
by freezing blades
Remote gongs
drawing us on

Flutes played
by droving boys
as they drive their buffaloes
along the dusk

5
Ropes give way
to ringing irons
as though I were decked
with showy rings of jade

The convict steps
with all the dignity
of an ancient court official
and all his restraint

6
Always the same bowl of rice
no greens no tea
Every man in this establishment
is at liberty

to wash his face
and give up tea
or take the tea
and neglect his face

7
The wife of a conscript deserter
has to say:

You left me
in our room
with grief for my only friend

So the authorities
took pity and assisted me
to one of their many gaols

8
Gamblers
promptly arrested
once inside
bet as they please

Can this be why
one so often hears it asked
Why the hell didn't I think
of coming here before?

9
Sleepless autumn night
no mattress
no blanket
the curled body

Moonlight on the bank
only deepens the cold
The Pole Star peering in at us
through bars

10
The sudden note
of one more in gaol
The note of the flute
weepingly swells

across rivers and mountains
and we seem to watch
her climbing that distant rock
to watch for our return

11
And one who was just
ounces of skin and bone

His end was cold
hunger and sadness of heart

Only last night
he slept by my side

This morning he has taken himself
on a frightening journey to the land of nine springs

12
Birds are seeking
the woods to rest
A girl in a far village
is grinding maize

When all this maize
is ground
the oven will
burn red

13
Ten years age you less
than a season in here
never eating your fill
never washing all over

In sum
          I have lost a tooth
and colour of hair
I have gained scabies
and a certain resolve

14
Poets used to sing
of snows and flowers
of moonlight and the wind
across the moon

Reaching today
we construct
poems in steel
and a poet's craft is to lead attacks

15

How each grain
of rice must suffer
under the pestle's pounding
to become so white

With man in this world
the lathe of misfortune
is turning us into
polished jade

16

Another hungry mouth
bites each night
at the right ankle
leaving the left sleepily to stretch

Stranger still
to clamour to be clapped in irons
and then be able
to sleep in peace

17

A constellation trails
from the summit
or the song of the cricket dies or returns
to tell the year

What could the prisoner care
what season it is?
Only for the spring of freedom
His and his people's

18
On release I walk in the mountains
the clouds hugging the peaks
the peaks embracing the clouds
the river gleaming as a cleaned knife

Along the crest of the mountains
my mind clears

I wander looking to the western sky
and think of all my old friends

ENTREPRENEUR'S PROGRESS

It having seemed in '68 a cool idea
to plant an unkempt traffic island

with 'grass' for harvest at night,
the suspended sentence taxed

the wit of red-top headlines
– TOFF SWINGS FOR ROUNDABOUT –

amused by his V to the rules
his kind lay down for us herd.

Shown on Personality shows
as a young meteor (meaning

a quick streak of attention
not the burn out and fall), that

was that; until he spotted
in the crack of a pavement

with dandelion, a few stalks
of alien barley in full ear,

a gesture planted to shock
for a sec the hurrying man.

A nearby poster was after all
already defaced, half torn-down

with its quote from Guevara, *Il faut
s'endurcir, sans jamais se départir*

de sa tendresse, and its assured
yet sensitive pen drawing

of an unbroken ear of barley,
the grain arising from the stem

as letters in a sensitive hand,
the tines of the nib gently splayed

to fill out the seed, then relaxed
to whisker off into a trailing line

the world now knows as his logo
stamped onto goods of every kind.

He started with us. He began
with paper packets of grain

given away at demo and festival
to take home and disrupt

that routine illusion of parents
going about their daily drudgery.

He never did find out which
hippy pacifist had drawn this his

perfect trademark, but once colour
supps had featured the brand

as a quirk for gardens bizarrely
involved with bootleg music,

he swung into orbit. Thence
the wholly natural cosmetics,

the expensive parodies
of market-stall knockoffs,

the no-frills conveyancing,
the private jet to private island,

the wives, the girlfs, the laddish
charm that got it off and away,

the creative accounting, the teeth,
the brilliant bankruptcies, the tax

frauds of THE ANARCHIST KNIGHT,
the very SPIRIT OF FREE ENTERPRISE.

RESPONSE

That we are all members of one another
as a theorem of Set Theory
makes complete sense to me.

TO LIVE BY THE BARRACKS

1
is to live beside monks
going about their secret ministry

2
Are those camouflage leaves
in slashed cloth
not a version of pastoral?

3
From their side all the mortar looks in order
From ours it sloshes
as though from the layers of a failed cake
and we grow climbers against our berlin wall

4
That extensive square
is now a car park for the invalided-out
with a rail for officers to rein their horse

5
On Open Day
a little boy within the armour plate
fiddles with the joystick of

a Rapier ground-to-air missile launcher
and finds the optic quite easy to unscrew

6

Tanks always 'roll' across the plains
            into other nations
                        and through their sullen streets
until this machine cranks up with a clank
shriek and harsh gnashing of gears

7

Today we have daubing of vans
Start at top left with a black blob
Then a sausage of murky green
Proceed to alternate these forms
Until bottom right is attained

whilst on the stray of common land
an entire friesian herd
huddled black-and-white under hawthorn shade
                        disruptively presents
a target all but invisible

8

Totally deaf since that explosion in Cyprus

We greet by thumbs-up

9

Once a soldier always a soldier
First a prisoner then a soldier
Then a prison officer
            he had thick lenses that magnified his eyes
I suppose you were kindly as you could be?
Oh no, he said, we broke sticks
across their heads
            and tears broke into his enormous eyes

10

In this cloister where unknowns are planned
they are planting out a parade of bulbs

11

At the gate with its black arrow slits
and amber level of alert a tramp shambles up
asking for the nearest caff
        A sentry with an iron-sighted L85A2
automatic assault rifle poking from his shoulder
brews the old chap a lovely cup of tea

12

                    Set back amidst mature trees
                        an unmarked house
                        with high blank gates
                        closed by keypad

13

The immortal blackbird struts along the shed
uttering her alarm
because a helicopter is screaming to land

14

And nearby roads called Stables
Love Lane
Hospital Fields

15

Of an evening
a red light at the tip of a radio mast
                        the sacred heart of Mars

IN ENGLAND NOW ABED

I concede that my comparison between
the crumpled sheet across a double bed
and the mountains of Afghanistan
was superficial and unworthy of either.

I can see clearly now that a bed sheet
is a single layered, relatively light weight
topologically continuous
soft and flexible fabric, whereas

rocks are many-layered, crushingly
heavy, fractured, sharp and brittle
although their properties may change
and, under unwitnessed pressure, flow.

It follows that those long ridges stretching
between summits like ideal snowy routes
would collapse, the many overhangs
would break under their own weight

and that I must retract my futile simile
made in the frightening light of dawn
which meant no more than to be aghast
at the map they face, their boys and ours.

FARGATE

In Fargate, Sheffield, where the Dutch florist
sets out his tablets of colour like a strict
field planted by Mondrian, a Burmese woman

stands entranced at blue waterlily heads
one to a flask, in martial array

I can taste it
    now. Mother
        used to send us

in a rowing boat
    to gather lily
        roots from the lake

I am leaning
    over the side
        plunging through

flowers to grasp
    the ever so sweet
        slippery stuff

We'd chew it before
    it ever got
        to the kitchen fire

Floating like lilies my sister and me

IN·TIMES OF PESTILENCE
Quoting The Decameron

When the Black Death came scything through Florence
Boccaccio had his ten narrators
in islands of villas whiling away
the greatest ever boxed set of stories.

When the same angel winged into Cambridge,
Newton holed up in a manor house
and spent the time under an apple tree
forming his universal idea.

It is a plague year but nothing occurs
to me. The buses go lit but empty
while 'cattle come home to their barns at night
without keepers, as though rational beings.'

FROM A JOURNAL OF THE PLAGUE YEAR

Round about now, the clocks change.
Carried over in our diary from year to year,
your note reminds me it is now
that uncontrived woods on the cliff
over Roche Abbey in Maltby Dyke
are sprinkled with wild daffodils
that escaped when Capability Brown
brought to order the rest of that ruin.

They are to me as deprivation was
to Cistercian monks who sang.
We'll not be going to look for them.
We have declared it Spring and stuffed
the chimney with a bag of crumpled
news as though a time capsule
because we'll be having no guests.
Soon enough, clocks will change back.

ON INTENSIVE CARE

Although at first the tangled tubes and wires
That snare my body, my own pulse displayed
In lights and numbers, would bewilder me
And I felt helpless, lonely and afraid,

I know that I am kept alive by these
Untiring gadgets, each one standing in
To breathe my breathing till I breathe again,
Machinery as sensitive as skin.

What is more truly dignified than this
Ingenious defiance of despair?
Such kind precision is a vital sign
That still connects us through intensive care.

DISTURBED HABITAT

Demolished, a rubble hill of bricks
already colonised by ash,
bramble, birch, coltsfoot,
it is in our lifetime that the Works
flourished and died. On its concrete floor,
outline ghosts of machine footings
are stencilled in black oil. Bald
groundsel roots in a crack with steel
shavings that once curled from a lathe.
Hardest to wreck, a lift shaft
is left standing, stripped of its floors
like the square tower of a hill town
in Italy, sprayed with graffiti tags,
all that is made here now being art.

The chainwire fence, enmeshed
with butterfly-bush sans butterflies,
lets to an abandoned steel yard
where, racked on railway sleepers
distinct gauges of rods and plates
lie coded in their dabs of paint.
There is no hammering, no
drilling, timing, lifting noise.
Nor are machines the only ghosts.
Sagging rafters of a factory
like the ribs of a rotten ship
fly a DANGEROUS STRUCTURE flag.
On its façade can still be read
'SUPPLIERS TO THE BEAUTY TRADE.'

RIPOSTE
After Franco Fortini

And now you write to me out of the blue
To say the air in your town on the hill
Is so dry and cool, even as the year
Draws in, that it seems a place to live
Into old age, the climate and the aches
Held in check by thick stone walls.

What prompts this? Who are you these days?
Perhaps all you need to be told
Is that you live on in your reedy laugh
Or by some other quirk in the weave.
Why send me word that a dry geranium
Stalk is scratching just now at your sill?

We had set out, you and I, with slight idea
Of which truths the wind would ask of us;
Or that the countless quarriers
Built in to those safe walls of yours,
And so much work of trees gone into them,
Would one day come to us for the reason.

How free the space then seemed; how strange
The paths over the bald hills into the wind
That had so little to drive against.
We saw the world in our own image
And our parents as unfaithful to us
And them – of all people! – as bodiless, alone.

Because of this the world has turned away
Its face, and we could not be perfect
Or even precise. And yet you laugh
And I can see you distantly in the disc
Down there in the well of our century
That has drawn down so many of our kind.

And so I walk with you among the dead,
Forebears in us of restlessness and words.
And I call you friend amongst the living,
And from how much experience. It was this,
I tell myself, that those ferocious winds
Were about, as they tormented the gardens.

III

I

Bees in hay. Buttons of ox-eye daisies
have been swelling like bread. First, outer rings
of interwoven spirals, a pattern of florets
that children score with dividers into a desk.
Rising lastly the compact centre, a dimple
of yellow pollens. Where bog and boulder
give to scraps of hay, the crop will hold
rushes, grasses, traces of every yellow
and purple, even the early purple orchid.
All the mowers have been pausing as I go by:
whole families will rest on scythe and rake,
gaze as simply as plate-camera portraits.
Then on again, lifting tossing and raking,
the hay cocked into beehive shapes
capped with squares of sack or fishing-net
weighted with stones, rounded in the jagged fields.
In raking light at evening they are impressions,
the bright edge not outline but haze
glowing with accidental lights and weeds.
And I, living still in the age of doer
and done-to, brought in some of the daisies
to make ink-and-wash sketches of them.

2

Through a gable window
inset like a box
in whose whiteness you
cupped eyebright stems

diagonal dawn will go
bringing to light these
brushmarks on the wall
tints in the counterpane

the shady slopes of our
female foldvalleys
and picking out the fleckle
of weeds in skin like hay

blue and yellow florets
and a spire of loosestrife
that is to eyebright
cold and outward brother

3
Needless radio-warning of gale
coming in force ten from Atlantic fast.
Children huddle in doorway, each a head
taller than another, watch sunset driven.
Looking at sun in its orange sheet of light,
emerald afterimages lie in the field.
Smoke hesitates, comes back inside.
Sea heaping. Long shatter-crested
waves foam, are blown into white streaks
along the direction of the wind. High, heavy,
toppling, tumbling and rolling over in shock.
All night this long overhanging crest.
Morning, and the bay as smooth as the pool
in the mouth of a candle, cormorant mirrored
fishing in it. Patrick was round for milking.
I started to chat about fiery sunsets.
'Is that so? We don't notice it round here.'

4
The *Irish Times* reports 'Heavy rain
has hampered the saving of crops in the West.
The saving of hay is delayed. Grain is lodging.'
A woman lugs a pail of waterlogged turf.
A lanky farmer, cap down on his brow,
pacing morosely up and down the lane,
growls at his children. Walls hardly emerge
from all the stones on the glacier plane.
One by one (as stars come out the longer
they're watched) the eye finds barn and figure.
Wait and feel. Half-hidden by the wall,
he walks unhurriedly through the rain.
All these lines written in steady rain.

5
Mist as the sun comes through grows more opaque,
dissolves. A family hard at the hay:
three men pitching high their bundles,
scowling, sweltering, drinking from tins of water;
children and grandmother fixing weights.
Then I came upon Patrick forking his hay
from a cart across the breast-high wall.
He lurched the two wheels out again
across the infinitely subdivided fields,
Patrick, with two quiet signs for the donkey –
halting it with a click, start with 'C'm on'.
Without this from him stood hard on its hooves.
He stood on the cart rummaging the nest,
I pitchforked the bundles up to him.
'You've never done this work before?' Nervous
of stabbing, I pitched hay into his hands. Later
he tidied round with a rake, spreading any
wet straws along the wall, to save them.

6

What did he think, himself, of Connemara?
'Lonesome in winter. You need a guitar.'
I tied a rope too loosely across one load:
he did not tighten it, but quietly added another.
Few from England: 'the Troubles in the North'.
At the time, I thought I was finding facts:
marches to Dublin over rates and prices
(but that was big farmers, not his interest),
the fine garden you'd need to bring in machines,
first a haycutter then a forklift on a tractor
counterweighted with stones. We worked and watched,
and as I write, as I remember your real name,
standing in the drizzle in your stony field
in the slanting light, feeding your calves on milk,
inhibited in your shy grace, calves
rattling their heads in pails among the stones,
I am sad we kept so many questions from each other.
'C'm on.' The donkey nodded towards his home.

7

Crossing their yard of erect geese for milk
that evening, I found the cart stabled away,
Patrick shaving from a basin by the sea-door
(the white verge on his wind-burnt lips)
and a newcomer's feet set squarely in the kitchen
by the glowing turf. A second cousin from Boston
who locks and sweeps up at Harvard, but
America had made him no less shy. We turned
to the weather, the critical sunshine. Could I help
tomorrow? 'But it's a Holiday of Obligation.
Don't worry, the weather is always given.'
The day after, then? 'Thankyou, the neighbours
will come in to give a hand. They're very kind.'

8
Fifteenth, a day of sunshine but of rest.
A holy day on an island with a holy well.
Phrasing of farms on other shores of the bay.
Mustard seaweed lolling at the waterline.
To write and eat at the same table.

9
'You'll find no language problems in Ireland',
says the glossy mag of the Tourist Board.
Irony withers, can say nothing at all
about Patrick with his indivisible word
based on the Gaelic for each thing he tells.
I'd learn from searching to speak so singly
who write a letter despising the tourist split
of weather by philistine wish – 'rain as usual'
or 'a good day' like an undemanding child.
Is it not written that the very stones shall be freed?
That is, from being bought and sold? Grey
is endlessly varied, a live and subtle creature
of rain-shrouded mountain, sea and cloud,
but that image supposes a freedom. 'Rain'
cannot be itself so long as it ruins hay.

10
Lying there out of ourselves
whenever this shower
came on, the early gust
throwing a handful

of grain at the window it
would take us back to – a hiss
on the sea began it – the
thin tiles becoming

that weather, this touching
as the pane melts as I
don't see it freezing ever
though seed be thrown

at a loss, and we not even
our darkness share,
listening for, later, the
soft fladge of rain.

11
Those perfect cocks, feathered two days before,
were cracked now into one great rick
that rose in a garden crammed with its making.

A skinted old man with straw in his hair,
two farmers, and a skinny lad in braces
– friends; not a penny of wage-labour –

were come to give their hands to Patrick,
his uncle and the Harvard maintenance man.
And Patrick received the pitches of vital hay,

smiling as host, and talking on all sides
in Gaelic, this boy I had thought shy.
Laboured with fork and rake, pitching and combing

until his mother in scarlet headscarf
crossed the fields carrying potatoes in her apron
and they lay and rested by the wall.

Boston muttered, 'I call it the old style.
Has always to be the same shape exactly,
as though a spell against the slashing storm.

'The West's a poor place to make a living.
Her children are scattered over the waters.
They call Boston the capital of Connemara.'

Setting to again; one on a ladder took
the bundles, handed them on to Patrick
at summit smoothing hay in rings about him,

knelt there in a cone twice the height of a man
with knees and knuckles kneading it into a loaf,
keeping all in touch, with musical phrases;

in this way his haycock found its rise.
A fuchsia-skirted girl passing in the lane
stayed at the wall to watch him, graceful in the sky.

The ladder hoisted off the ground to him,
he stepped back in neighbouring fields to see
how shapely against the wind and rain it was;

then, combing away the slovenly strands,
taking it in at the base and choosing stones
from the wall to fasten sacking, the lad with twine

coming in, the cock alone in its garden
next to a garden with a single hobbled cow,
Patrick patted the work and said, it is finished.

Fragrant the hay, from the lane in the fine rain.
In the yellow light and the scent of new bread
Spilling at night from their door, his hay stood.

AND ALL WENT TO BE TAXED
For Barbara Garvin

A city of stony fields, reticent people,
the thornbush stunted slanted by seawind
any driftwood going to gate or roofing slat
the smaller gathered for kindlingwood

Strangers noticed a mile down the road
children hiding from a strange lorry,
on watch as the periwinkles gathered
by them in sacks are weighed on a yard

Men talking in huddles by a stone fence
blocked with flotsam, seeming to strangers
close as shellfish, closed as axioms
lidding their pipes with bottle-lids

String from a parcel will go to hold
a gate together, the new sacks the grain
comes in will dampcourse a bale of straw.
Turf, ricked neatly as the turning slane.

A yard of fowl have their grain scattered
by children clucking and calling pet names
to a granite slab that crops up in grass
as the lined palm that bases the cottage

As the mother keeps knots on every thread
and just now sets a geranium pot
in the red-silled window in the thick white
walls that keep their secrecies like ferns.

The candle grains the limewashed stone like wood,
being the strongest light. Drawing its watchers
as in dawn or evening light, the shadow reveals,
bringing to fabric what our affection brings,
converting sight into a touching sense,
as it is the raking light discloses
the painter's gesture and repented form.

Candleflame in virtue of its weakness
will search like fingertips the patina
as written as a hand, worked and worked over,
the skindeep scratches and workings-even
cracked and filled, smutched and smoothed-against
in the crust of lime with insects bedded in
and the fossil of a paintbrush whisker

enhanced now by the obliquely feeling light
as it casts the grain, resolving the room
to a reddish-yellow order that has the art
of graining stone like a working tabletop,
turning the shadows to a rippling sense,
a handscape falling out with authority
by its love of all that is variable;

and such the walls return, each granule
within the glowing body of the recess,
as though their width were made of nothing else
but mild candlelight, composed of flickering,
edging onto the window's geranium lip and at this
familiar horizon cutting to black, to pulse
across that wide unsearchable where it is not.

And there went out a decree
that all the world should be taxed
and at first the Jews cut up rough
but the blind overseer calmed them,
Joasar the highpriest, explaining
'the necessity of the arrangements'
that they be taxed on salt and meat,
work the land for the foreigner
and render on the roads to Caesar.

Yet there was one Judas
of Galilee, who saw a census
preparing for Roman tax prepared
for enslavement, and nations have
to assert their freedom in arms.
No man should submit to mortal man
as Lord, nor should the word
of any taxgatherer be honoured
nor his testimony any more.

And this Judas asked the Jews:
What are you talking in whispers for?
and whether, if there could be any
amongst them put up with declaring
for such a tax, they would declare
anything but their cowardice.
And this Judas was able with such talk
to gather many people after him
and light a candle amongst them.

So it came to pass that for his
'inviolable love of freedom'
this Judas was executed
and all his sons; and their rebellion
gave to Jerusalem for the first time
an entire Roman legion stationed
to retain the City of Jerusalem,
and the number of the crucified
amounted to some 2,000.

And after that, says Joseph
ben Mathias called Flavius Josephus,
one brutal war came down upon us
after another, and we lost our friends
who had used to soften our adversity
and there was pillage and murder
of our principal men, whence arose
further seditions, and murders
which fell sometimes on the enemy.

And then the Famine came amongst us
that brought us to despair;

so it is not to the doorstep preacher that people expect
for the springs of former content to be running again
the wilderness and the lonely place to blossom with shops
for the Galway road to be straightened out
the stones of Connemara ironed out
like creases from a shirt

for the sailing boats to be fishing the islands again
for the Bens to be made low and the bogs of Ireland drained
and tended with gardens with fruit between the rows of fruit
and the farthest islands bridged to the main
the deserted islands roofed and returned
the long divided joined

nor for the voice of the Gaelic to be heard through the land
nor yet for the prayers of the living to be empowered
to rouse the dead
                          and bring the scattered home
as we dream the ones who are lost and gone
are home and swimming in the rivermouth
and in the breaking wave

as candle light

is touching down across the stony fields
and even out to sea, received as harbour light,
and any reddish star is clinging to the coast
as lights in network are strung around the bay,
making tracks between clusters and outliers,
reflecting the fishing-boats lit like a village,

so many candles interlacing haggards and lanes.
The mild flame in the four-paned gable window sees
to what height the rock can be pressed into bearing,
traces the contours of shepherds, mountainy men
keeping their sheep inland, and the crescent of bedrock
of glowing islands in line with the coastal hills

a tally of candles and all that goes searching in them,
as the outlandish appear from slope and bogland
hidden by day, and watchful children at windows
point them out by name, to the farthest window,
even the newcomers, even the guards, picked out
by candles, by children, by name, like so many stars

on January the 5th, Eve of the Epiphany,
when the real cold weather begins
and hay to be forked out into the fields
when the head of the house would pound
the bread of adversity
against the windows and barred doors
that Famine might pass them by that year
and when the next harvest is the sea rods
and some admiring candles watch the sea,
sensing night that offers its coastal taste
in fifty modes as subtle as snow or sand,
to turn the shadows into a rippling sense.

On January the 5th, Eve of Epiphany,
Twelfth Night of Christmas, Nollaig na mBan,
Anniversary of the Big Wind, the windows each
to each recover flickering connecting lights
along the heights from Coillin to Calafinis head
and to Finis island and Muigh Inis
and from Coillin to Leitirdeiscirt,
Roisin a'Tomha, Carna, Siduach,
and Ruisinnamainiach and all the world
of Iorrus Aithneach constellating itself
to itself as it goes with all the world to be taxed.

IV

THE QUICKENING

A child cups a moth
in her hands

'It tickles!'

To hold is to hide.

Forgotten for years,
until the quickening

when her baby makes
first move.

ETHNIC MONITORING

The well-meaning form requires
my tick in a single
                        box for your race
so many fields compressed in a bud.

You went searching through the vaults
of a vast library
                        to borrow your sequence
some of it latent for hundreds of years.

Who cares if these are your father's eyes?
or your Viking hair
                        a raid on Lincolnshire
or a white African settler's trait?

Did the Mongol invasion of Norway
give rise to your
                        epicanthic folds?
Are these thoughtful fingers

those of a Jura watchmaker? Whoever
could have dumped
                        your infant grandpa
on a Leeds doorstep? Vain questions now

we can print out the long involved spirals
of heredity.
                So, familiar stranger
ticked as WHITE OTHER, I gaze along

escapingly subtle curves of your brow,
the bones of your skull
                        continents drifting
together. I exult that you have fetched

your codes from every quarter, and that
so many variables
                compose your
secret head. I kiss your fontanelle.

THE SLING
For Eloise

It is trying to snow.
Having been ill, my fingers
are thin and white.
The baby slung to my chest
is a clinging monkey.
I am all wrapped up
in her sense of comfort.

LIFE MODELLING

A toddler won't hold hands
but latches onto a single finger
tugging it almost out of joint.

A mother, grateful to pause
and show this lavender bush
seething with bumble bees

has to press on, one arm braced
ahead to her pushchair, the other
back to drag her child up the hill

so as to set that ascending line
for The Unknown Mother
in some heroic monument.

ON A JANUARY MORNING

In the bright crown of a leafless oak
in blue sky at the turn of the year
a song thrush breaks into song.

I brood on Hardy's darkling hope
and those strange lulls in trench warfare
when birds reclaim their territory.

Excited children merely exclaim
how high it is, how small but loud
and 'I can see its little mouth.'

SKETCH OF A YOUNG MUSICIAN, INTENT
For Zoë

The line of your chin along the rest
reflects the body of the instrument

but not exactly, so as to hint
a tension crouching over the score

A grit in the charcoal catches
lips in fleeting subvocal twitch

Beneath the breathing of the strings
you concentrate and count

ON A PEBBLY BEACH

When our family was young
and the children took off over the stones like little dogs
as we followed in our different conversation
and the game was, to come back with the Best

it struck me that grownups tend to select
those that the sea had spent her centuries of energy
smoothing and buffing
from rock until perfectly formal, the ovoid, the oval

but our youngsters go for the grotesque,
the knobbly ones with fractured faces and funny holes
that can have fingers poked in and out of them
or look like puppies or gulls

and now that I sleep diagonally,
and walk alone on this beach,
it is truly hard to decide
whose preference was the more mature.

Leafburst in the limestone valley,
everywhere stippled with points of colour.
By a gate in the drystone wall, a shy
four-year-old is urged by her Gran
to take off today that woolly bonnet –
'It's her cling-to-me thing.' All of a

sudden a damburst of bellowing cattle
surge through the field from corner
to corner, cows and their rust-red
calves in high excitement – 'dancing'
the old lady says – as the father on his
quad bike watches from the crest.

'It's their first day out after winter –
First day ever for the calves –
Shorthorn and Highland in hardy
cross – My husband brought them
here when we started – Any smaller
calves would be trampled to death.'

What is the child to make her own
of this bawling sight through the gate,
this stampede of fresh clover,
this cow jumping over the sun,
this festival force of sheer release
and the dialogue of the comfy hat?

MY SON FOUND A COW'S PELVIS

As I say, we were out walking and
my son found this gigantic bone
and by hanging it around his neck
it fits him! Archaic breastplate
of a science-fictional Knight.

Walking grew tedious, not least
from bearing of pelvis on chest.
He thought he might hitch a lift.
At this point my experience
came into its own. My dear son,

one thing I do know about is
hitchhiking. Let me tell you,
no one'll ever pick you up on a hill.
And there is no verge to pull onto.
And this is a minor road: no driver

knows where you're thinking to go.
Place yourself at a major junction!
What's more, you're begging strangers
to let you into their car despite
wearing the filthy pelvis of a cow.

At which point a tractor drew up
and took my son I know not where.

SON OF GRIEF

If asked which *National Geographic* I most regret
not having filched from the dentist's waiting room,
I should without hesitation reply: the one about
cricket, as she is played in the Trobriand Islands

those benighted savages having been taught
by Methodist missionaries the shame to be felt
in nudity and rude ignorance of cricket and Christ,
with the result that those pacific, photogenic folk

to this very day, having feasted, play up the game
kitted out in bright-feathered penis sheaths
and vary somewhat the ritual rules with cries of war
and war dances, and retain on each team a thirteenth man

a marauding jester suitably undressed, whose sole duty
it is to jape about and taunt the foe and sledge
the crowd and send up the whole event. I would like
to tell you more, but just then I was called – not, alas,

to the Ministry of the Church, but in to surgery;
yet how often do I muse on those colourful shots
and the difference such reforms of the game
might well have made at my Methodist school

where I found myself forever on the boundary
counting (methodically) in a sample square yard,
how many spiders, beetles and such small worms
were also striving to carry on their lives on that ground.

ANCIENT FLOWER FORMS: GENUS MAGNOLIA

Almost everyone walking through the magnolia grove
in the Botanical Gardens will take out their mobile.
If alone, they snap a close-up of some selected bloom
and instantly move on. If a couple, they will take snaps
of each other against the blossom and may spend a while
head-to-head confirming whatever it is they have seen.

A daddy taking out his little girls is now phoning
a single perfect flower. His daughters are picking up
fallen petals, pink and pulpy but already rusting
at the edges. They hold them up to each other, using
them as fans, antlers, floppy ears, fairy wings until
a squirrel shows up and a girl goes chasing after that.

The other stands as still as she can; it approaches her.
It is she who discovers she can write on these petals
with her fingernail and that her scratches will soon turn brown.
And yet, who am I to prefer the less boisterous girl
or my own peculiar lens as I stroll through the grove
to observe magnificent petals preparing to fall?

IN SPATE

The clear brook that used to trickle through the woods
conversing with its own valley
is now in full dark peaty spate
throwing aside whatever it will not bear along

its current sucking the ground from under fast boulders
and hard-rooted trees
breaking out and filling fresh parallels as it cuts itself
into a deeper bed

so that in justice to my heart-wounded daughter
and the forces rushing through her
      fiercely crying herself to sleep
I cannot say be at peace

BY DERWENT DAM

Lolling in the dead of summer
    on the bank of a reservoir I watch
       a boy skimming stones
A few skip once and quickly sink
    mostly they sink at once
       and it looks just lucky when
a stone bounces along like a bomb
    and with the boy Coleridge
       he 'numbers its light leaps'

With no more knack than his
    in duck-and-drake affairs
       I think I can easily see
how he might differ his angle
    select his missiles and govern
       those clumsy energies
except that even as I watch
    he's picking up his own tricks
       and fewer tries go down

       utterly into that reservoir
    made by reflected woods
and by drowned villages

CALLING JAMIE

Helloo! Jamie! Jamie!
You've Wo-on!
You can come out now
The game's o-ver
Brilliant hiding!
We can't fi-nd you
You are The Win-ner
Well done Jamie
Clever, clever, boy!

It's time to go ho-me
It is getting da-rk
We're going home
Come out Jamie
That's enough now
It's time for te-ea
We've got to go home
We've stopped playing
Come along please

Or we'll go without you!
It's alright Jamie
Are you all right?
No one's angry
Don't be afraid
The hiding's over
Please Jamie please
We're still he-re
We're all getting cold

We never said
We'd go without you
You are our clever boy
You won the hiding game
Can't you hear us
Calling your name?
You can come out now
Wherever you are
Ja-mie! Jamie. Jamie?

V

THE GRIFFIN'S TALE
Legend for Baritone and Orchestra

The griffin is a rare example of a flying quadruped. It is easily recognised by its lion's body and its eagle's head, wings and talons. A Griffin's capacity for air freight is as large as its ferocity. Marco Polo heard of one breaking up an elephant by dropping it out of the sky.

The word 'griffin' came into English through a fourteenth-century poem about King Alisaunder, also known as Alexander the Great. This Alexander was a fabulous being, said to have lived in the fourth century before our era and to have conquered the whole world as then known to the Greeks.

Alexander's legend started with his taming of a famously unmanageable horse. Observing that the animal was alarmed by its own shadow, he faced it into the sun and was thus able to calm and mount it. Learning thereby how simple it might be to subdue the world, Alexander set about uniting it by force of arms under Hellenistic ideals. These were to be instilled by gyms and other facilities in a dozen cities, all named Alexandria, where he demanded the kow-tow of prostration and kissing the ground – gestures properly due to a god.

Nonetheless, there was a reflective side to Alexander's nature. He interrogated any local sages that fell captive to him, and pestered oracles wherever he went. Visiting Diogenes, he enquired whether there was anything he might bestow on that barrel-dwelling philosopher. 'Yes there is,' replied the Cynic: 'you can stand out of my light.' The conqueror remarked: 'Were I not Alexander, I would be Diogenes.'

Another of Alexander's fantasies was aerial reconnaissance. He built ladders and hills with which to survey battlefields, as well as venturing on a celestial journey powered by one or more griffins or great carrion birds.

The following witness has been collated from the most reliable sources in mediaeval romance.

GRIFFIN:

It was a dismal summer, all green and quiet.
We hovered by crossroads, hoping for carrion
            And squawked and squabbled over the helpings.

But then one day the pickings were good. Herds of brutes
On horses clashed and bellowed as they slashed their skins.
            A rosy glut of guts was unhidden.

Peace fell. Such thew and sinew. Such spicy giblets.
And blood as thick as dung. No time to fight – no time
            To wipe your beak. That hour was our finest.

Feasting lulled me. I was resting my head in a
Ribcage when some ruffian clambered on my back.
            It took three or four hops to eject him.

I sank my talons into another fetlock,
But more of these featherless bipeds flung out a net.
            I fought! Lopping and chopping about me.

Useless. They wrapped me in ropes. Then their beast-in-charge
Came to inspect, his rabble bowing and blowing
            Kisses from their claws. Here's what he boasted:

ALEXANDER:

The sky is leaning down
        To meet the earth. The sky
Unrolls its bolt of cloth for me to step upon.
        I am the one to whom it falls
To quell rumour and survey the field.

Just as I bridled the wild horse
        Maddened by its own shadow
By forcing him to face the sun, so now
        I steer my gaze to the heavens
And defy the oracles.

My historians will echo:

        'It was then that years of research
Into bubbles and rockets
        And scaffolds and special hills
Delivered their terrible seed.'

        Therefore:

All these entrails –
        Interpret them.
Make farthest sightings.
        Predict conquest.

Abandon work
        On Hills of Surveillance
Take ironmasters
        From the Star Staircase

And carpenters from
       The Towers of Foresight.
Abort the artificial wings.
       This project has priority.

Let a carriage be built!
       Mount spears at the corners
And a harness on top
       To be drawn by that creature.

His are the wings to haul
       My ship of the air.
Let the hull be strong.
       Make a porthole for me.

For it is my will to see
       As the eagle sees
When he sizes up terrain
       So as to seize his prey.

GRIFFIN:

Well! They kept me awake with their saws'n'their hammers,
Drills and chisels, and they kept me starved. Otherwise,
       I was well treated. Sir, the guards called me.

Then at dawn they breathed on bits of wood, made them glow
And – listen to this – stuck four sweet suckling piglets
       Onto spears and teased them with fire

And sizzled and scorched them under my nostrils,
Turning the dripping grease in the dangles of smoke
       That bore the squealing smells to my senses.

Then, they chained me to that botch of a chariot
And their overlord came back and all saluted
      Him with one raucous voice:

                          A– le– xan– der!

Next, this Alex loaded himself in the cockpit
And fastened his belt, and I could sniff them fixing
      Those key-babs to the roof at each corner.

The stink was delicious. A hot splutter of fat
Splashed on me pecker. I could stand it no longer.
      Famished, I lurched the job off its moorings.

In ravenous craving I launched it spinning into
the sky, twisting around the winds of the colours
      of space in a lust for those piglets.

I hoisted higher, but no nearer them skewers.
Ice formed. My quills prickled. Alex was shivering.
      The earth looked like a deep-frozen eyeball.

Hailstones flashed past me. Reeking above me
The meat was still crackling – and as for the cargo,
      I could hear His Nibs muttering prayers:

ALEXANDER:

Nothing, nothing like I thought
       The black air meeting the starry poles
The whole world, as never before

       Spinning in a dark immensity
Our tiny world of time ...

How distant my armies
       My splendid horse
How vain the cities bearing my name

       How trivial
My athletes, my engineers

The whole world and its islands
       Passing under my view
A walled town with civil gates

       Fringed with terraces and herds
Meeting utter wilderness

An oasis with its palms and fish
       Receiving trade in wine
Resin, salt, copper and slaves

       From far away across the sand
Beyond any map or hint of good rule

And I laugh to see
How vastly small
Are the accounts of men

Their courtship, strut and pout
Their petty quarrelling

For the liveliness is just as full
In a seedpod snapped
Open by the sun, or

Deep among damp leaves
In the green gulp of a frog

Above all, I can survey
Sea-road and battlefield
Crops, enemy emplacements. Yet

It is the little fly with paper wings
That captures my gaze

And the bulrush by the stream
The tendrils on a vine
The stripy spirals of a snail

And the day of a man
Swift as the hawk's rapture

And always curling around all of this
       The ever-encircling sea
That slowly pulses in its coil

       The world – is a threshing floor
Surrounded by a snake!

But there, there is a river meandering
       For thousands of marches
Through ramparts of mountains

       And there a continent
I could break with a mile of canal

There, a plain of tameable horse
       There, timber for hundreds of ships
There is a precipice, yet at its foot

       The lakeland, the tract of pasture
The vital source of supplies

There is a mountain spurting fire
       There an impassable glacier
There a forest surging with rain

       And there
Is the crucial pass, the way into Persia

GRIFFIN:

At this a man-like shape with skinny wings and legs,
Nothing to peck at, popped up from behind a cloud
And (all Greek to me) started announcing:

ANGEL:

Yes, there it lies. A threshing-floor
Where many flails thresh and thrash
          To nourish the kingdoms.

A threshing floor coiled about
By its blue green snake. You see it there.
          Just as you wished.

You pitch your tent on the field of the world
And it yields to you. The world is your City:
          Alexandria. But

Remember Xerxes and keep in mind
You are of earthly woman born. Raise not
          Your head too high.

Now you see it all and know its boundaries.
Know then your own. Turn back your spears.
          Avoid the gods.

You run the world, you, a glob of spit
That runs about hot iron and makes a fuss
          And, hissing, disappears.

You wear a helmet, you wear a crown
You will be told the truth by a naked old man
    Who lives in a barrel.

GRIFFIN:

So. There I was. Desperate for a slice of pork,
Chained up to a wooden crate in the stratosphere,
        Icicles hanging off of me gnasher,

With some kind of general who was embarking
On a Greek dialogue with an angel. Food for
        Thought's the one thing I just cannot stomach.

So I clawed back the situation. I hurled us
Into a giddy dive, peered in at the pilot's
        Personal porthole'n'gave him a beakful:

Angel-face does have a point, you know. May not have
Much lard on him, but his guts are in the right place.
        Let's get home, eh? Thin air's not for eating.

Think of all the flocks of the world throwing back
Their throats for your fangs. Think of the armies –
        All that flesh gone to waste, such a pity.

Or if innards don't tempt you, think of the kingdoms.
You could have a bit of clout down there, I reckon.
        Let's make a survey; won't take a moment.

But his Highness was still aloft in his raving:

ALEXANDER:

... Now I see it all
And know my place. The narrow
    Sphere of the earth
Must limit my conquest ...

GRIFFIN:

So I tried on a spot of the old soothsaying:
Where is the profit in these islands of the sky?
    You shall gain Persia! Think of the Glory!

That did the trick. He steered down his piglets and crashlanded,
broke the whole box into a pile of planks.
    I flapped away smartish. It made me croak

To watch all his animals rush to devour
Their leader's remains. No more feasting, no more blood
    For that wingless gob called Alexander.

VI

ALEXANDER TO CHARON

Here is my coin. You know the face
That sent you cargoes of shades, in my day.

A SHADOW LEANS AGAINST A TREE

There is nothing to be thought
I gaze at a broken bubble fixed in the glaze of a mug
He'll be going into theatre just about now
The key to the box is locked inside the box

In the beechtree's pool of shade
A few hailstones are not yet melted
Hailstones with dog violets
A thing my friend may never see again

MY STRIKE-A-LIGHT

*On the Isle of Whithorn on the Solway coast of Galloway,
excavation of graves from the early mediaeval period turned up
a smooth white quartzite pebble the size of a hen's egg. Scratches
across it show that it had been used as a 'strike-a-light' for tinder.
The pebble had been buried in the grave of a child.*

My little light
My strike-a-light
My spark struck off
A sharp old age

O bright and likely
Shining girl
O true, O white
Most lively stone

Here is stone
My only lightling
My stricken mite
So sparky one

AT THE BARBER'S

Mr Scott used to work at the chair with the best light
and a view of the street to keep an eye on regulars
as we went about his business of growing our hair.

If we noticed him as we passed he'd raise a scissor,
patient that we'd soon enough be back through his door.
Well turned out, his own hair low-maintenance,

a soldierly looking man, I thought he'd outlast me.
Epochs of daytime television passed over his head
as he'd clip, chat, and keep a watch on the street.

How're the children doing? I still call them that.
How's the mother getting along? You know how it is.
How many grandkids does that make? His restless

motion back and forth round the back of the chair
was continually wearing out a grooved arc
not only through the lino but into the very boards

as though he might drop like the cartoon fisherman
through a hole he'd sawn for himself through the ice.
I didn't know he'd gone till I saw the new lino.

THAT DAY AT KING'S CROSS STATION

That day at King's Cross Station we forgot
our journeys, were caught in a silent ring
round one man pummelling another's heart,
heedless of the spreading pool of piss.

It seemed a visitation by some truth.
Even compassion was held in suspense
as travellers were forced to contemplate
the breaking of the mortal instruments.

What must a painter see to realise
how people stand around a martyrdom
until the ambulance slowly withdraws
and attendants come with their mop and pail?

FROM WHERE I STOOD

From where I stood at the foot of the bed
at the moment of death, his body lay
with heavy chest and all that drapery
like Mantegna's Lamentation Of Christ.

Subdued by the murmurs of monitors,
his mother first and then the rest of us
gathered about him in a single thought,
his pale head slightly turned away from ours

so that each of us assumed by nature
those postures religion pounces upon
and paints just when we are helpless in grief,
so as to claim and foreshorten our man.

Oak leaves and catkins are fluent again
along the branches you no longer see,
your mind and mine held forever awry.

Struck by a curious line of poetry –
my first thought being to share it with you,
were you not mining inaccessible seams.

I hear a son's concert in his father's name.
We knew both musicians. Where were you?
Involved in staring down a deep stairwell.

How to reply, when you told me delight
had drained from painting and only cows
are content to chew on landscape beauty

and music itself was turning ugly by
a labyrinthine disease of the ear?
We spoke of the Heiligenstadt despair.

Had I been with you to stare down that well,
would I've asserted Beethoven kept up his fight,
or laid down my thoughts along with yours,

or tried to restrain you? You have your own spark
I could not stand by and watch you snuff out.
About that I am not stoical, nor will I cheat

by taking us back to those catkins as though
recurrence can feel like renewal. I set myself
to think, as did you, how to stare all this down.

Which sounds too much like a last line.
I hope I could simply have stood at your side
so that you were not quite so finally alone.

IMPROVISATIONS

Children, hostage at Beslan, allowed
no water, stopped from drinking from lavs,
were laid out in bags in rows in their gym
with letters, flowers, teddies. Families
placed by each one of them a plastic bottle
of the very water they had been denied.

A London busdriver randomly murdered
on duty, the funeral march of strikers'
banners and brass band were led
by a double decker that he had driven,
as though the riderless horse of old,
its destination scrolled to black.

Transparent once, yellowing sellotape
dries to release its bouquet of words
from the streetlamp of a roadside shrine
so we know there was somebody who was
stabbed, run over, or came off their bike
here. And reflect more finely on our lives.

WINTER WALK

In memory of Jacques Berthoud

Making our way along the thin scarf of mist
that clings to river thorns, a farther line of trees
a grey comb knotted now and then by nest or mistletoe
or some such canker, the only colour being
iron of dock leaves and rusty wire, he pointed out

a group of farm buildings, outbuildings
and an old wall rounding that previous way of life
and told me he was minded, come the spring,
to return and make a water-colour study of that
pleasing cluster of forms, were it not for certain

bleeds of iron that could make all this tenuous
as a wisp of fireweed, spent, adrift in failing light.

The dead have no landscape, tense or mood. How can
the phrase 'The Dead' refer? There is no 'They'.
Their being in the Past is logical, but even so their nouns

betray us with a sense of continuity that cannot hold.
He or his name is but an empty sign. It evaporates
from that which it would signify. Nor are there names
reigning over us to save from renouncing words
for beings that we know unreal; unlike the present mist

loosening from other matters this bank of thorns
where he could sparkle in talk of suchlike paradox
and where, as I hold in mind as evergreen, my friend
took notice of skeleton leaves, tincture of rusting share,
the composition of that farm and its retaining line of trees.

WRITTEN UNDER THE WISTERIA
In memory of Astrid Berthoud

       Under the shade of this twining vine
one could sit and look back on the house
from the foot of its long garden and reflect

that the plan had been sturdy, the pergola
firm to support what had to climb
around us to build this arbour of years

and we read her careful signature
of pruning to express the flowers
and persuade the form of their bower

sometimes following best advice,
at others a whimsical snip or weave
of a whippy shoot back into the thicket

of stems which then thicken to branch
and compliantly recall and entwine
a moment's decision into the tangle

of interlaced angle, plash and plait,
each snaking, each harsh truncation
the consequence and living fossil

of someone's thought and action
in long forgotten states of mind
with outcomes, often as not, unforeseen.

Pausing in clearance of the house
to look back once again from this
translucent shelter of memories

I take a long look at the building
from a kitchen chair which itself
is to be one of the last things to go

and study whatever plan or impulse
had been going on there; how the force
of growth will accept and harden choice.

It is not even the annual mass of bloom
but the sombre writhing of leathery stems
that is the really remarkable sight

though May is the obvious floribundance
of dangling of thousands of densely
sweet peas that cluster like so many grapes

therefore best time for estate agents
to picture the house in its peak of allure,
graced as it is by a mature wisteria which

moreover, is sited at the foot of a long garden
that abuts onto a side street, so that this shrub
is easily grubbed to make room for a car.

ORDERS OF BURIAL

Driven from the city to its rim of hills
that give onto the distant plain,
our black cars slow to walking pace,
make sense of the gradient slump
so the body knows we are going down.
At this, having been lost in our thoughts,
we think we've arrived, look around,
but vista has straitened to a narrow lane
descending close domineering walls
as though we tunnelled into a pyramid.

The convoy issues at the foot, the same
slot of horizon now defined
by black avenues of cypresses.
Family alight and set about their work.
It feels wrong, glancing back to observe
how the trick had been engineered.
Behind us, severely parallel walls
concrete-buttressed against the slope
like the flume from a dam, had cast
the extreme cleft that had taken us in.

For those of us still able to leave,
the original route's never taken again;
that remorseless mock defile,
that bodily sinking, has caused
once and for all its ennobling fear.
Here we shall rent his brief plot
and return every year to touch, to kiss
the enamelled photograph and leave
every tint, from white to orange to rust,
of chrysanthemums to dry in the sun

until the very last day for which
the cheque was signed, whereupon
his remains are unearthed, crushed
and pigeonholed into an ossuary
tiled with numbers and names,
whom I last saw in the hospital
and, lightly on his temple, kissed
when he asked that the reading lamp
over his pillow be switched off by me,
murmuring *La piccola luce... Spegni.*

CONVERSATION

As I walked past a caff in a strange part of town
you tapped on the sweaty pane to beckon me in
I sat down opposite as though an expected friend

The shadowy youth at the counter did not stir
his gaze transfixed by a plastic orange damned
to float round and round in its drum of watery juice

I asked, How're you keeping?   *Could be worse*
You're a better colour   *Got over the jaundice*
How are they treating you?   *Not bad, considering*

Get anything off for your service?   *Not a day*
Same as the pension fund. You pay all your life
and it's nothing but snowflakes settling on water

Not lost your turn of phrase then   *That I did*
give you   You always told me the cost of your gifts
(and in this silent conversation, I silently weep)

When all's said and done, I taught you to speak
and read and write with stories night after night
'and my profit on't is I know how to curse'

I even gave you 'red plague' with my flash
of Trotsky   You watched me take down that book
but never came clean whatever it meant to you

Too late now   Apparently not   *(Silence)*
I was too harsh   Now you tell me   *(Silence*
The same sterile fruit going round and around)

How long has it been?   *A whole generation.*
And now you're a father yourself   Yes, despite
the 'sins of the fathers' you used to preach

It took me a while to work out what that meant
It took me a while too, by the way. Every so
often I catch myself echoing your words

or tones of voice, or carrying out some action
of yours. The crumbs on this table, for instance
you'd've swept them with the side of your palm

off the table to the cup of your other hand.
From that you'd give them to sparrows, thus!
Just look at those sparrows, squabbling in dust

I have to be going, there's a hole I have to dig
I think we should forgive each other
There are things that go without words

No, don't weasel me, it's far too late for that
How you were, was part of a history shared –
which is the only sense I can give to 'forgive'

There are certain things that go without saying
Speak those uncertain things, or how can I know
you feel, for your part, there's ought to regret

or whether I am forgiven also? A word would...
When all's said and done (which it is, by the way ...)
Brimming with silence, he had almost said...

when the youth sauntered over and presented our bill
Few meaty remarks; no drink; unspokens on the side
It came to so many snowflakes settling on water

LOOKING AFTER

They've spread from the dense oblong
we'd intended. Crocuses
infringe
on neighbouring beds.

We take our time in weeding,
in ritual watering,
and think
on their names, their dates

in our seasonal visit.
Crocuses encroach again
and so
they will always tend.

AN HUMBLE PETITION TO THE FAIRY OFFICERS

Well into the last century, Irish country people had an explanatory framework for mental 'alienation' that was at least as coherent as anything proposed by the medicine of their time; namely, that the afflicted person had been exchanged or 'taken' by the Fairies.

Potent bewildering kindly Sirs,
Inspirers of springs, hidden lords
Of milking and crops, arbiters
Of sea-peril and in music supreme;

We, a family at wits' end, entreat
Your honoured ears to our petition:

That, after such interval as may please
Your Graces, you graciously restore
Our child to his family and powers.

As to our boldness in addressing
Your high persons, we can only plead
We have been at every pain to consult
Philosophers wise in such things

And not one has a better thought
Than you have spirited our son away
To enjoy your hospitality awhile;
So great, so undeserved a privilege

That, grateful, we request you name
Any consideration in clinking coin
Or buttermilk or finest flour of oats
Or eggcups brimming with potcheen

To be left by whatever threshold,
Well, lost shoe, thorn bush
Or rare isolated flower that you
May be pleased to designate.

Have we offended your ways,
Be gentle to clarify the cause
And resolve amicably; for
Do we not live on the same land?

We have already knocked, stone
By stone, our most recent barn
Lest it had unwarily blocked
Some natural lane of yours

For this, his family, truth to tell,
Is pining with grief to see him again
As once he was, charming, self-
Possessed as you have him now.

We are growing to accept it may
Please your Excellencies to prolong
The honour of his sojourn with you
For a far while yet in our time.

You will find him clever company,
Knowledged in the kinds of fiddle;
Just ask him to chat about his cat
Or traveller's tales in democracy.

May we, however, with respect,
From out of merely human hearts
Invite you to weigh in intellect:
He was not raised in your world

And may hanker for primitive ways.
His father, mother, sister, friends
Yearn for his pleasing fellowship,
Wherefrom we fully appreciate

That your Graces will be entranced
By his comely discourse and person
Who may even begin to think
Yours is the world he wishes to live;

And yet, discerning as you are,
You may come to tire of human style
In horsehair drawn across catgut,
So unlike what it has been our luck

To catch, on rare evenings, floating across
The stony mist, faint sound of, your
Ingenious music in solemn revels
At respectful distance from your fort.

His dancing figures may be strange
To you as glimpses of yours are to us,
So might there perhaps come a day
When your Reverends, now entertained

By your curious courtier, feel surfeit
Of his society and, in your noble tact,
Enquire whether he is wholly content
To be so away from his own music?

May your gentle natures pardon
Laughable clumsiness of form
In little folk approaching you thus,
Our being illiterate of any court

Or cogent precedent likely to move,
Or proper manners to address,
Such authority as yours, deferring
Solely to your rights in the matter

Which is to us no less than the joy
Of our dearly beloved young man

Whom we have the temerity to implore
That you may give us leave to hope
That some day without cloud or omen

Just as he disappeared, we shall see
Again, smiling and playing on his violin.

VII

ON THE FELL

Winds have
so cut it it
can give
an edge
to wind

a sand
stone
boulder
sandblasted

to a blade   a breathless bone
releasing these   sharp grains   of sand

CONNEMARA WALLS
For Eoghan Ó Tuairisc

Walls, a maze, like cracks
in glaze on a discoloured plate,
trail away to hazy distance.
None surveys these boundaries,
the criss-cross ways of walls.

Lazing as iron-bearing rocks,
bullocks are sullen in their gaze.
A donkey strays, a living slab
of the granite-grey, grazing on oxeye
daisies; suddenly splits

in brays the softening mist.
And always the hard sea, halted
in crescent bays, is heard
as it flays the massive shingle,
preys on its long-lost bed.

A breaker sprays: within the tide
big boulders concuss and daze,
splinters blaze in sunken sparks.
Yards away, a farmer lays a wall
of these nearly erased forms.

Sunset rays pierce the wall;
days are edged with lace. Colour,
going to ground, is raised from dull
duns and greys into grace
and plays in the setting of this place.

DISTRUST OF LIMESTONE: A GROTESQUE

There was a deep unearthly boom, home shuddered,
Tree went into shock, and what we half-know could happen
      But not here, not thinkably to us, occurred
To Lucio and his twentyseven goats swallowed up
      With the collapsing land. Immense and sickening,
The chasm gaped in an olivegrove where no mines ran,
      A jagged mouth of darkness that without sound
Continued to consume the thrown or odd falling stone.
      Water was guilty, and underlying beds
Full of faults, they taught the village with its awkward sense
      Of sin that for decades tried to fill that hideous pit
With all the rubbish it deserved, until this madman
      With a torch in his forehead tackled the black,
Pried the sidecaves, mapped the fossil river's treachery
      Roofed with farms, and traced its every furtive stream.

So olive gnarls, revets of prickly pears, a few figs
      And that vast sinkhole could now be sold off cheap,
The groves grubbed, the spot refenced, the great gap
                              rimmed with brick,
      Generations of peasant refuse hoisted,
Bats shooed out, making for stairs on an infernal scale
      To publish this debris of drip and ooze
– *It is cold underground. A pullover is advised,*
      The turnstiles clack; *No graffiti please. Respect
The work of millennia,* the souvenir booths respond –
      To let the adults dabble in abandoned
Levels of desire, browse the instinctual archive, reading
      Madonnas, towers, but mostly vegetables,
into limbless draperies of unwondering stone.

Are clammy kilometres of kettle-fur
Truly various? The cold millennia exude
        Slimy veils of their random limestone stuff.
Crowds trudge the vague metro, sucking icecream stalagmites.
        Yet the tourist knows what has been built of this
And what its kilned cognate can cement; what furnace it,
        Being deadburned, lined can fuse; what wings may run
On ways that it hardcores. And what the confused sibling
        Decorously recollects in letters cut
On white surfaces that shameless sweatless feet have crossed
        More silently than wood, deeds later limelit;
And of the poisons following in cylinders on trains.

        Cavers and climbers, visitor of mother
At weekend, addict of unsuffering aerial view,
        When will our zodiac mottoes urge: Live up
Nor down to nothing, but praise the Ego's witting plane,
        The dense turf around the world, intensified
By almost all the talking that has ever gone on,
        Crafty knowhow of canvas and dovetail joint,
Level crossing, fanvault cavern, Lucio and his goats,
        Glass houses and scant relation to plans,
All canals, most striving for effect, just about all
        Conduct of meetings, blood donors, floppy disks,
Innocence until proved guilty, the Great Vowel Shift –
        By the fertile layer of party tricks and forms
Of government, artificial beauty of the fields,
        Moveable type, the overt stream's reluctant
Tribute to the undercourses nibbling at our crust?

SCENE IN TUSCANY

It is spring and in the thin leaf
the grain of every thing is more distinct.
    The parts of corn, hardly in shoot,
leave their furrows clear. Fringing rushes let
    streams flow right up to their edges.

A dove flops into the pock of a wall
    of a fortified clump of farm,
tower, and one-room church with curly tiles.
    Winter's hay carved to the spindle,
a whole lemon tree stunted in a tub,

    watch the valley and opposing
slopes, violet folded hills calm as lips
    in the slight mist that varies tints
misty but never mixed as they come down
    to olive thickets and blond clays,

taking up scattered pieces of young crops,
    gingery willows in half-bud
fuzzing to a bit of a pink orchard
    and a bit of white freshly pruned,
fluttering rages to civilise the birds.

    It is morning; the labourers
can be picked out among trim lines of stakes
    moulded to the valley contours,
tying the as yet leafless vines that comb
    to sky-edging dabbed with small trees.

The details are being trained, buds chosen.
        To every tendril its clipping.
A black-shawled woman bundles the snippets.
        Olive brishings heap by the path
as symbol of the season and its task.

        The thigh-stump of a polled willow
holds taut the twine for shoots of this vintage
        to creep along, its own shoots cropped
for the twists of springy twig, skilled device
        clipping the young to the old vine.

A shiny cock is standing on a wheel.
        Scrap, shred, wisp, wedge, strip of colour
is intrinsic as leafing bud. It is
        almost time for Western landscape
painting to begin, its long displacement.

IN THE PUBLIC GARDENS, BORDEAUX
For Joséphine and Marc Dubreuil

    Gilded gates make a sprightly
entrance to one of those spaces
once noble now democratic, as open
as any we have, a 'field full of folk'

The *petit peuple* have been let in
beggars even, even the distracted lady
led about by kindly keepers showing
her to her delight the ring of girls

delightedly linking hands like girls
torn into being by dextrous hands
for an absurd paper chain to mock
surrounding statues' classical pose:

    That Arcadian shepherd leaning,
lest he snap at the ankle, against
a goatskin spread on a stump
tootling on his throttled flute

ignores his modern avatar
bearing a bicycle wheel to be trued
yet both gain entrance and those
rectified persons, those of note

in virtue of their stones, assume
a quietly overgrown place amongst
the paths and threatening sprigs
of which Nature used to remind

Rain upon stone has for so long
revised the youth whose marble
puberty must wrestle forever
with his own Chimera to retrieve

his lyre, broken between her claws ,
– Oh amorous allegory! –
for a statue cannot take a statue
into its arms as a sculpture may.

Nevertheless the sinuous rivulet
continuously giving back the gaze
upon such flexible dreams
will reflect our mingled thought...

That look so fixed within the trees
of solid worthies resigned onto
their plinths, and those deliberate
buildings, yet afford a certain play

as though formality might not
after all be the only power.
Walkers on terraces perhaps
linger to gaze on playpen dunes

Practical lovers on the bench
can park their pushchair by
an exotic specimen tree
that stands them timely shade

Those infants trapped in a tent
witness all the political science
of puppet theatre and thrill to see
what they could never wish to see

An orator denounces acid rain
to an elderly gent, a puppy
and an Algerian mother dangling
a fluffy ball for her child

Slick suits confer by phone
for all the world as though
these public gardens were again
the *bourse de la soirée* of old

That couple back to back
in the bole of a tree may read
one Éluard, the other D' Alembert
Such poles of feeling seem

natural here. The swan regards
the drag of the bank with ripples
of disdain. Then (although the gods
no longer to confide in us) a clump

of chestnuts towering above
the roofs just now gave out
an almighty crack. A branch crashed,
stilling the entire space. Nothing spoke.

ASKED BY MY MOTHER WHICH OF MY FATHER'S THINGS I WOULD LIKE TO BE GIVEN

The arrow head. You know –
that ivy flint-leaf he
told us he'd found in his youth
climbing Inkpen Beacon.
Just spotted it. In his path.

It must be somewhere.
A triangle of black flint
you could fit on a ha'penny,
daintily flaked, with tang
and barb nicked into the base.

I think him alone, don't imagine
his 1930's rig
or even his face. I am within
that vigorous day of skylarks
views and unsought finds.

Never mind; I have it already,
my sense of the instant
his anecdote was knapped, shot
and lay to be found. Give me that.
It's that has the barb and tang.

THE BEST EXCUSE I EVER HEARD

was a poem in itself.
                        My chameleon
adapted herself to our Persian carpet
so that my sister couldn't see it and trod on her
so that I had to take it to the chiropractor
and that
                    is why I couldn't come to your tutorial.

MEMENTO

Between the pages of Victorian poems
I find this fern, pressed like one of those
rusty fossils in yellow sandstone layers
that open like a book. And I wonder
how she came upon that object lesson
and thought to leave it in a poem
about a waterfall and endless loss.

WINDSWEPT SEA

The costume of Rumour
covered with tongues

HITCH-HIKER'S CURSE ON BEING PASSED BY (EXCERPT)

The Curse of Your Wheels to you!
May your inlet manifold get choked
While your head gaskets are leaking
And may your camshaft lobes wear out.
Although your cylinders each crack,
A man will be found to replace them,
Wrecking as he does so your valve stem seals
And knocking your tappet clearances awry.
No fruit of your driving: your plugs never dry,
Your tanks never wet, nor those of your daughters.
Trail a long lorry loaded with logs.
Speeding to get you nowhere, slowing down
To bring you neither calm nor safety.
Stones to puncture, sheep to stand stubborn
In your path, dull bulls to dent your doors
As ever forking lanes confound your way.
May your turning left end all at sea
unless into quicksand, your rights into mines
Or else onto firing range. May you backfire
And blow the crook from the fist of St Pancras
To bring down all His curses on your neck.
Seven terriers to snarl at your inner tubes.
Rest at last in a black bog, whereupon
A slide of boulders to bury your wheels and you.
Crawl, you may as well, up your own silencer,
For be assured: you will come by no agony
But that you will survive to suffer it,
Your fate a mystery to your own people.

AESTHETIC

The rippling of reflected sky
on the underbelly of a boat
sets other thought aside

SURFING THE MOVIES

> *I used to enjoy dropping into cinemas with Jacques Vaché,*
> *no matter what was showing, at any point in the film, and*
> *leaving at the slightest hint of boredom, only to rush off to an-*
> *other cinema where we'd repeat our performance.*
>   – André Breton, *Comme dans un bois* (1951).

The police are in the act of being about
to ask questions later. She plucks his lapel,
kissing to test his breath. Intercut
police are still saving their voices. We hang
about for half a reel, then pan next door
only to find the same music-lover
passing an overweight viola case
to his business partner, whereupon an effect
of bleached Mozart causes him to fall
in slow motion past many storeys of glass.
Cutaway to street, stop down against
the glare. We find ourselves another dark,
two language-users riding the surface
bareback to exit on a slow dissolve.
Don't take it personally, advises the next
usherette as she tears our admissions in half
winking to the screen goddess already at work,

the lily-of-the-valley evolving at speed.
Strictly speaking, nothing moves in flicks.
That last footage threatens to be the end.
Neither is about to splice, neither is a woman,
but they hold hands in a grainy nimbus with
an orange as point of reference, the orange still
contriving its elements of the truly expected.
We have stripped beginnings of privilege
but that first sequence of the afternoon,
the one with the little boy with large eyes
and nasty secrets, set some kind of tone,
making it harder for posterity to resist
orangepeel that blinks from the gutter which
'is our conductor rail!', Jacques proclaimed
as we hastened along to the next fleapit.
All that velvet, that involving drapery.
All those tasselled enveigling loops.
We fled before they had a chance to part.

PICTURE

Under a grey mountain
        a grey lake
                with its lonely skiff

and the painter's flowing brush

TO THE LIGHTING ENGINEER

This is not a theatre
so we have very few lamps.
The way to play it is restrict
even those that we have.

Wind down that rig.
Lower that ceiling still more
so as to sketch in coal
an adverse area of dark.

As a proper stage can afford
to sing its aria of light,
we are forced to give over
most of ours into shade,

shadows, musicians
beggars playing in and out
of such light as is granted
to characters like ours

as marked by Doré
the black and white poor
lit infrequently
by police bull lantern

or shone up for show
in magic lantern slides,
but for most of history
out of light out of mind.

To grant relief
from dark spotlights,
all other lamps
being spoken for,

let us devote a single bulb
a colour-gel a
meretricious peach
for the tango scene

and look to that glow
to play upon couples
by way of its glittering,
its revolving ball.

ON A CERTAIN POET

That silky cat in a single elegant phrase
draws out the syntax of its motion so as to leave
clear each object cluttered on the mantelpiece it slinks

along and between so as to cause no catastrophe
to obstacles acutely observed and yet untouched,
leaving things pretty much as they are.

A SPOT OF TIME

———— Be that as it may.
The summer also held a livelier theme
And germ of brighter thought. Unlikely source
Though school exams will be for youth's delight,
It was a text – of all things, a Set Book –
That put me to the study of my heart.

It was the year that Kennedy was shot
And other scenes, uncannily, were stopped
In their procession to forgetfulness
And burned into our memories of where
That news was shown. So, in a flashbulb, I
Can forcibly recall the very fence –
The traffic noise beyond, the quiet here;
The standard oak or gnomon of the day
Whose patchy sunlight, sunlight-mended shade,
Would cross our lawn; likewise the kitchen chair
I shifted through the hours as I read
The Prelude and its power was set in train,

For then it came upon me in a flash:
This verse of language, this is wonder-full.

REFLECTION

The young woman opposite me in the train
        reads a book on the art of poetry.

Would our lives have been so different
        had I known then what she is learning now?

A TYPE OF VENUS

As crouching marble makes
the goddess use her hands
elbows, knees and their soft hinges
draw attention to those parts
of her body she affects to hide,
so (the white line of stanza break

serving that simile) our art
must conceal its art although
not too well. For how much art
was made except by fighting shy
of those without whom not
one of us was brought to light?

ON A MINIATURE BY ANTON WEBERN

An initial letter
     glowing with knowledge

Exacting as light
     that glances about within cut glass

As exposed as a fact
     that gives itself no excuse

Yet close, open and closed,
     As the locket held to your breast.

MUTED LAMENT

I once heard an absolute of unaccompanied song
in a Connemara kitchen by that proverbial fire
and even then the song was all of long relinquished songs
fallen silent, furled alongside sails of fishing boats.

In an English drawing room I clap transcripts
for violin of impressions for voice of a set of folk tunes
and the convivial room applauds a rendering
of our own last echo of long-lost longings of our own,

for why should such a formal continuity not be
as moving as the oral stream? The strands of feeling
drawn from her voice evoke our wish to hear the very girl
the violin remembers calling to the fisherman who vanished
                                                    out to sea.

SEATED FIGURE OF AN OLD LADY

After Celia Paul's paintings of her mother

So still, your frailty becomes a monument.
It is as though I already mourn whom I protect
By drawing this thin curtain to sift the light for you,
Still in the window where you would write to friends.

The room is open at the page 'Help thou mine unbelief.'
You are sitting for the light that veils as it clarifies
And finds by variation all the riches of a single theme,
The artist mother bringing figure from ground.

Wreathed in the thought of children's faithlessness,
You can hear from the yard that the blackbird sings.

AT THE THEATRE OF MYRA

Why does that ancient voice,
the colour of sand and sun,
gurn a dumbbell infinity sign?
To make a Mask of Tragedy,
open your jaws painfully wide
and, holding that, strain to close
your lips across the silent scream.
Not by crying but through restraint
you have now pulled your face
into dramatic form. You possess
the trick and truth of it should need
arise. Eyes, also, scream.

ANNUNCIATION WITH BLACK SQUARES

A virgin and her angel of maternity
Staged in white unblemished space
Decree that any other image here
Be read as symbol, so determining
The kneeling suitor's formal flowers,
The prayer-stool lectern and the book
From which he is distracting her.

A virgin, angel, and between the two
A far landscape replete with hill
Or else, in ruled receding vista,
An enclosed garden, to recall
The future – these we receive
Within the tableau we compose,
Being formed by that very book.

But what to make of Veneziano's
Black squares, hung like paintings?
Although a tiny window in glaring sun
Can pierce its whitewashed wall
Black as a pupil, and window grills
Are brushed in oily lampblack soot
Within the strict frame of her cell,

Those enigmatic forms invade:
They are hard to read as natural
Apertures. Black-winged, strange
As angels, they come to announce
A picture is not what it depicts.
The human body is to be deposed
From the grid of its own aspect:

> **a black square**
> **declares a lily**
> **a lily proclaims**
> **a black square**

DUTCH INTERIOR

A lady in blue in her inner room.
A being that one fed on cactus might see
as an angel or pure concept of light.

The household knows a letter's arrived.

The cook has her eye to the keyhole,
having quelled the puppy with an egg.
On a cleanly tile, traces of eggy slime.

The lady hesitates to break the seal.

The maid, to show herself unslovenly,
swishes the floor. In the trail of her broom
the dust resettles itself into gentle drifts.

PROPERTIES OF VANITAS PAINTING

The child's globe; the descant recorder,
emblem not of deathless art
but mortal shortness of breath;

drosophila, that ephemeral
lab animal that flirts around
our bowl of ripening fruit;

the shard of clay pipe we found
in the soil, last touched by lips
of men who built this house,

kept on our sill as though
to remind we are 'but dreams
of shadows of smoke';

even the half-spent candle,
its melting tears at its flank
at the ready to time a power cut;

and my wife's skull, the one
she studied at medical school,
scavenged from some killing field.

But then the children's delight
at a dandelion clock shooes away
all my bats and owls.

AN INQUIRY INTO THE PORTRAIT OF
JOHN WHITEHURST BY JOSEPH WRIGHT OF DERBY

In memory of Mark Roberts, Conservator.

He is discovered in his study at night.
His astute, unflattered profile,
the hair thinned through tracts of time,
looks up slightly, as though to weigh
an idea that's just entered his head,
two other themes being lit: his work
overflowing the writing slope and,
through the window of his Grand Tour,
a distantly smouldering Vesuvius –
one of Wright's tenebrous Italian views.
Otherwise, timeless abstract night.

Such a tableau was easily read
by the worthies of Derby. It displays
a finding by their ingenious friend
who by dint of diligent reason
adds to the sum of useful knowledge.
The paint renders, almost to touch,
not only his gently capable face
but his thought: the crucial diagram
of local strata known to owners of mines
which they possess in copperplate, folded
into their fifteen-shilling quartos of

AN
I N Q U I R Y
INTO THE
ORIGINAL STATE AND FORMATION
OF THE
E A R T H ;

DEDUCED FROM FACTS AND THE LAWS OF

NATURE.

At last! a product from all those years
of listening to him at the table, his face
in candlelight, the clock of his own
making on the mantelpiece as he
sorted and measured his day
-by-day observations in Matlock;
Here at last every wheel is in gear
and this the great connection he drew.

He is discovered in deep shadow,
with not even a clock to suggest
the slightest sound, for this
is the primal scene, the fertile night
bringing unforeseens into birth.
The paper, the volcano and the man
are placed as in a waking dream,
all else in suspense. And, for a study,
no book is visible to show
the natural philosopher the way,
or the world how it comes to be as it is.

But, if this be illumination,
there is no saint or poet's eye in fine
frenzy rolling to inspiring source.
He is alert but level. He looks up
slightly from his work, to consider
a thought in distance out of the frame.
Oh, I see! It's exactly the way a painter
glances up to check their subject.
Wright, in depicting his friend,
depicts him as a brother artist
as he brushes that thinning hair.

In the very instant of insight,
the painter compacts his own volcano
with his friend's precise drawing
of a section of local habitat
prepared for the engraver's burin.
It is a painting about the moment
of thought, about art, about science,
and it paints about friendship.
It is a painting about the stubborn
intensity of loving attention
that may elicit concept from dark.

He is discovered in his study like Faust
in Goethe's Rembrandt frontispiece,
riddling forbidden mines of lore,
the toadstone nodules and the rifts
loaded with ore that conjure
rules of stratigraphy, vulcanism,
the subterranean fire, the inferno
indifferent to us as the planet revolves
within its clockwork orrery.
His book will clarify creation, the point
of his pencil turned to his own breast.

GUIDED TOUR

Here we are, in the renowned Spiegel Café,
scene of the last poem before he shot himself.
Yes, all these mirrors are great for selfies.

This is the actual corner seat where he watched
via those mirrors the demented gentleman
– Do grab yourselves a coffee while you can –

whom the regulars dubbed The Professor
who'd sit all day long with endless pots of tea,
soundlessly declaiming to his imaginary class

– and don't miss out on the legendary cake
drenched in liqueur, though in our poet's day
the Spiegel was, as it were, more bohemian.

You can take it in turns to sit exactly here
and I'll go round the corner so you can spy
on my reflection pretending to mime,

as in the poem, rhetorical touches of passion,
intense gazes from side to side of the room,
and the pause with courteous gesture to attend

to some objection unheard from the floor,
mouthing an answer self-pleased at its wit,
acknowledging murmurs of silent applause.

Or you can take yourself, if it strikes you
as amusing, in one of his dumbshow faces:
the sceptical eyebrow, the signature smirk

depicted in countless engravings that we
half noticed as children, regarding the past
as it was insisted upon us in those days.

And of course you see written on mirrors
in every language the final stanza,
perhaps a little pretentious to our taste,

about the mercurial mirror as the very image
Of such lucidity as may... But you know the phrase
And how, unless ironical, our poet claims

to envy that pathetic café Professor,
lecturing to thin tobacco smoke, his air
of simple-minded contentment with words

oblivious to any present audience. We now
have a few minutes to eat up and take snaps.
Then the coach will take us to look at his grave.

THE PATH TO COURRIÈRES
An 1815 oil sketch by Jules Breton

The gleaner in her shawl, the rough linen sling
at her waist, figured against the evening sky
as she returns to her village, is absent here;
it is the painter himself who trudges home
in the receiving dusk, his harvest done.

The place of the woman is held by the tallest elm,
its crown drawing a scatter of silent rooks.
The path leads the eye peacefully round
to the low houses, brick-red and white,
and to the church tower and beyond.

No hint of surveyors, trial drillings already
there at the time as exploitable veins
were opened and spoil heaps begun. Not yet
the coaldust explosion, the Kameradschaft,
the burning church, the massacred hostages.

Time has scumbled all that history.
I come into the gallery out of the Sheffield rain,
put down my shopping bag next to a bucket
catching the skylight drips. There it is,
its frame a little brighter gold than the corn.

I let my eye be led again by the curve
of the path to Courrières, past the verge
of poppies, the everlasting elm, the wheat
as permanent as Ruth. The rooks, chipped
into the paint, may never settle again.

And in his dream he hung all his work
Around the house as for a final show
The nervous portrait of a youthful wife
With her basket in their first garden
The studies of Welsh slate-workings
The abstracts the ultramarine phase
And the apple of his eye the series
He called Transfiguration

And found himself weeping that
No tomato ever tastes as it smells
Acrid on the broken vine and he was
Visited by William Blake who said
Nothing, noticed nothing but paint
Just gazed intensely and simply
Touched each painting ever so gently
So that it kept itself exactly as it was

In its intent yet completely fulfilled
Every stutter cleared every limit resolved
And he woke. But how did that leave him
To feel? Thrilled that Blake in person
Had blessed his art, or depressed
At alteration true geniùs made?
And he started another portrait of her,
Tending tomatoes in their garden in Wales.

WHERE'S THE POETRY IN THAT?
– as Archie Markham would challenge his students.
His pseudonyms included 'Sally Goodman'.

I bumped into your old flame Sally at the shops.
I was palpating an avocado when this hand
appeared. I knew her from that kitchen scar.
'Are they ready?' 'Ripeness is all', I quipped.
She had the courtesy to laugh, drawing herself
up into that lengthy Scandinavian beauty
you used to say was in so many ways like you.

I started to tell her how deeply I missed...
She started to say 'These days I scarcely exist...'
We lapsed into reminiscent silence.
We knew the other knew the anecdotes.
So I dared to ask, 'What did he really believe?'
'He believed: that Lucy Locket lost her pocket.'
With that, she faded up the Fresh Food aisle

leaving me still half looking out for you
bowling towards me with your dandy red
scarf streaming against the wind, drafting
to yourself the line of this morning's
sulphurous fissure, sadly provocative yet
true all the same, as in your saying 'And so
friends die to help us bring forth poems.'

VIII

TREE SURGEONS

Two men dangling in sky
as though on parachutes

shut down chainsaws
fasten their harness

in the chestnut crown
and raise their visors while

birds fall silent and
the sun suffers eclipse.

What is their chat
as a blue cave in a cloud

floats a white canoe?
What does each think

in hushed eerie light
as birds chorus again

and men yank at cords
to re-startle their saws?

FROM AN ESSAY ON BASHŌ

On a high lonely moor, tradition.

A curlew's call, curlew curlew.

The centuries. The morning.

That glint on a curlew's wing.

That exact mood of loneliness which is set up
between a frail creature or event
and surroundings by which it could well be overshadowed
but to which this very mood might show it to connect.

What is friendship?

A common taste in poetry.

SILVER BIRCH

Clear in cobweb,
wings of seed.
All over, in fact.

We tread them
into the house,
they sleep in our folds.

Primal woodland
here, did we die
or desert it, silver

birch would succeed
as though our kind
had never breathed.

VERSIONS OF *JISEI* WRITTEN ON THE VERGE OF DEATH

A dewdrop came and went
Once I governed Osaka
that dream of dreams
    Hideyoshi Toyotomi (1536-1598)

I have no house no wife no child
no wooden printing block
no money yet I wish for no death
    Shihei Hayashi (1738-1793)

Wherever has that dog got to?
I thought of him again
tonight as I came to bed
    Shimaki Akahiko (1876-1926)

INTRAFACE
For Edmund Papst

We come to the last garrison town.
A signpost: the English is painted out.
Beyond, Barbarians Begin.

Across that border all is borderline
a swan ends up with a salmon's tail
holding a sickle reaping the wings of a swan

One way the boatman rows, another he looks
Currents coiling and merging emerge and recoil
the weir an attribute of a two-faced god

January god of threshold and fresh start
Artist of loss, hesitation, sleep
A face inscribed on the back of a mirror

The otherworld begins to speak in touches
of broken rocks rusty with bracken
– these being the least elusive signs

We're losing time, Europe itself is ebbing
away as we cross the Shannon, travel
west like water slipping over a weir

The lost ones enter at the year's turning
show their face at a time of decision
and you, holding your sheaf of poems

Connacht giving facets of its grain as you
gave me a word, 'scatch', for hillside
roughage that utters a batch of thorns

A lichened boulder, the living depicted
with large and staring eyes that close
when they seem to belong to the dead

At a Janus gate but lacking his poise
the balance of alert and resigning face,
Let this be an active turning-point

A dream of a brimming tide on the turn
I see myself reflected in no child
Verbs of liking thinking and wishing

Let the other touch and change
the fish tendril into the bird
the word a gateway into the wish

AUBADE

Listening in white dawn
    to the kinds of birds
    and for all the song
that has been made of this

new light flickering through
    slight specks in the weave
    of curtains giving
to our bright coverlet

we know again what is
    about to impinge

Morning tickles the day
    into surfacing
    from its drowned valley
only to bring to light

the down of your shoulder
    green veins in your wrist
    ways you seem to have
trickling into being

with the morning and with
the fragrance of sound

Seedlings begin again
    The room is opened
    by tints of almond
alive to this moment

frail corals of light
    steadily building
    patches of detail
on the hand on the quilt

Filtering curtains gain
    again their effects

Despite its nervous ways
    light's no animal
    nor looks down on us
with savage moral will

It is in our own eyes
    the white or as yet
    vaguely dark shall find
their eventual form

and the day ask of us
what we make of it

METAMORPHOSIS

From Ovid or Bernini one might think
metamorphosis a gentle melt
of one into another form, as though
through animated film from frame to frame.

Not so in nature. There the animal
eats its own innards, discards live limbs,
shatters working tissue so as to burst
out of its beauteous tegument.

Daphne, morphing to laurel, her pulse
palpable even now through the bark,
is out to trash inheritance

so that, violent as any thought
of Darwin's to our doctrine of fixed kind,
a fresh creative form may erupt.

CYPRESS: AN ODE

The shrine is encircled by tall cypress trees
And out of that soil a profusion of springs
Flow silently. There Apollo stoops to bathe

And there a sapling grows that once was a youth,
Cypress by name. It is the beauty of the tree
That makes the transformation plausible.

– After Philostratus.

Here is no shrine to transformation; even waterfalls
Fall silently; enchanted glades
Are no defence of verse where pilgrims quest
For changeless verities;
Yet we travel to disclose our homeless thoughts
Where cypress trees are silhouettes of flame
That scorch the underlying streams to flow unsplashingly.

As for the youth so casually calm, unshouldering
His backpack, encompassed by trees
Of exalting height, breathing unbreathed air
In the spring of his day,
Already a portion of that which merely
Being young entitles him to, he stuffs
A plastic bottle into the cleft of a tree, and pees.

A second celebrant or nymph of this place comes bearing
Vegetarian sacrifice
In a floral basket of her own weft.
A third is plucking at
A homemade pentatonic lyre. None the less
A sapling thrill arises from this ground,
And shades that nurture our wish for flamelike changes of form.

In the eye of cold philosophy, a tree will take shape
After its own repeating style
Written in almost immutable code
Forever conifer;
The comely God Himself, descending to bathe
Was merely a fanciful way to see
Nothing more than reflected sun as it sets in a pool

Just here, the very place where it is said that He implored
Sad Cypress to set himself free
From an inordinate grief, having killed
The creature he most loved;
But Cypress was growing already within
His own body that sweeping bronze-dark tree
He was soon to become, arrested in its weeping spire,

For did he not unbend from his trunk the bristling limbs,
Splintering his skin to unfold
His cancer or his travesty of birth
In changing loveliness,
Stabbing, splitting his grieving self inside out,
Then to absorb his needles from the floor
As he expressed himself as an emblem for any grief?

Although the deeply enfolding shade goes on lording it
Over us, subduing our thought,
We begin to notice a few ripples
In this black-green water,
The lyre retreating before the weir's chuckle,
And teasing reflected glimpses of sky
That we'd never have seen in inwardly reflective trees;

So we're able to take our leave of that enchanting place
And drive away through verticals
– A cypress grove by gloomy yard of graves –
Transected by distant
Diagonals of white turbine blades fringing
Bright plains of mechanized sunflower fields,
Thinking from time to time of Cypress, his beautiful tree.

ACKNOWLEDGEMENTS

Barbara Garvin helped me with Franco Fortini's Italian, and the poet generously approved our versions. Keiso Shimuzu provided cribs from Japanese. First printings were acknowledged in the books from which these poems are selected. Amongst the seventeen new ones, 'On Intensive Care' was a project at the Chesterfield Royal Hospital. In the original collections I also acknowledged various critical friends and audiences. For this selection, Judith Woolf kindly checked the text and caused me to make a few corrections.

'A Swallow', 'The Griffin's Tale' and 'Aubade' were written to be set to music by David Blake. His scores are published by University of York Music Press. 'A Swallow' can be heard on *The NMC Songbook* (catalogue NMC D150).

*

From *Tidal Models* (Anvil, 1980) are drawn the poems on pages 32, 34, 38, 64, 129, 132, 139 and 166. From *Our Worst Suspicions* (Anvil, 1985), 16, 24, 30a, 42, 43, 72 and 130. From *Eventualities* (Anvil, 2013), 26a, 27, 28, 36, 39c, 40, 53, 56, 57, 61, 80b, 83b, 86, 89, 94, 106, 107, 108, 115, 120, 128, 134, 137, 144a, 146, 147, 158, 168, 171 and from *In The Event* (Carcanet, 2020), 23a, 26b, 30, 31a, 31b, 39a, 39b, 41, 50, 52, 58a, 58b, 80a, 82a, 84, 87, 88, 90, 91, 109, 112, 116, 118, 123, 138a, 140, 142, 143, 144b, 145a, 145b, 150, 151, 152, 156, 160, 162, 163, 164, 165, 170.

The following poems have not been published in book form: 23b, 35, 59, 60, 82b, 83a, 85, 110, 111, 114, 122, 138b, 138c, 140a, 140b, 148a, 148b, 159.